"This beautifully crafted book sets the religious writings of Lewis within the context of German idealism and English Romanticism. Barbeau brilliantly draws upon the marginalia in books from Lewis's own library to place him within the tradition of Methodism, the poetry of Wordsworth and Coleridge, and the philosophy of Schleiermacher, Hegel, and Feuerbach. In the construction of theological language, Lewis is revealed afresh as a deeply learned, sensitive, and serious Christian thinker."

David Jasper, honorary professional research fellow for the School of Critical Studies at the University of Glasgow

"Jeffrey W. Barbeau's eloquent and accessible lectures look past the blinding assumptions of standard intellectual history to discover a modern C. S. Lewis inspired by religious Romanticism—a vital, creative tradition of poetry and thought that unites the subjective and objective, the personal and the divine. Lewis's place in this visionary company was there all along, expressed in his stories, essays, self-representations, and previously unpublished marginalia. Thanks to Barbeau, we may also see that Lewis, like Elijah on Horeb, was not alone as the last inspiring, faithful Romantic."

Michael Tomko, professor of humanities at Villanova University and author of *Beyond the Willing Suspension of Disbelief: Poetic Faith from Coleridge to Tolkien*

"As a scholar, Professor Barbeau does not disappoint. He has done remarkable research teasing out the degree to which C. S. Lewis was affected by the English Romantics, which he says was pervasive and primary. His style is winsome and engaging. Did he make the case? Let the reader decide. I must say, I enjoyed the book and discovered some things I had not seen before. It is a good read!"

Jerry Root, Lewis scholar and professor emeritus at Wheaton College

"There are so many books on Lewis that are simply a rehash of existing knowledge; by contrast, this is a work of fresh, detailed, illuminating scholarship. Barbeau's work on Lewis's long, close, and intimate reading of Coleridge and Wordsworth has unveiled new depths and even given us a newly discovered poem by Lewis. Barbeau dismantles the clichéd idea that the Romantic element is mere subjectivity and shows decisively how Lewis's 'Romantic' engagement with intense personal experience actually dovetails with and reinforces his arguments for the objective truth of Christianity. Barbeau's use of Lewis's personal annotations in the books in the Marion E. Wade Collection is a revelation and makes this book a permanent and important contribution to the study of Lewis's thought."

Malcolm Guite, Life Fellow at Girton College, University of Cambridge

"*The Last Romantic*—a bold claim about Lewis, yet one that Barbeau fully supports with fascinating detail—offers not only the best guide to Lewis's engagement with the Romantics, it is also a wonderful study of Lewis's thought and faith in general, as well as a wise meditation on connections between modern theology and the Romantic imagination. Enter this wardrobe and you will not come out the same."

James Engell, Gurney Research Professor of English Literature at Harvard University

JEFFREY W. BARBEAU

WITH CONTRIBUTIONS FROM
SARAH BORDEN, MATTHEW LUNDIN,
and KEITH L. JOHNSON

THE LAST ROMANTIC

C. S. LEWIS,
ENGLISH LITERATURE,
AND MODERN THEOLOGY

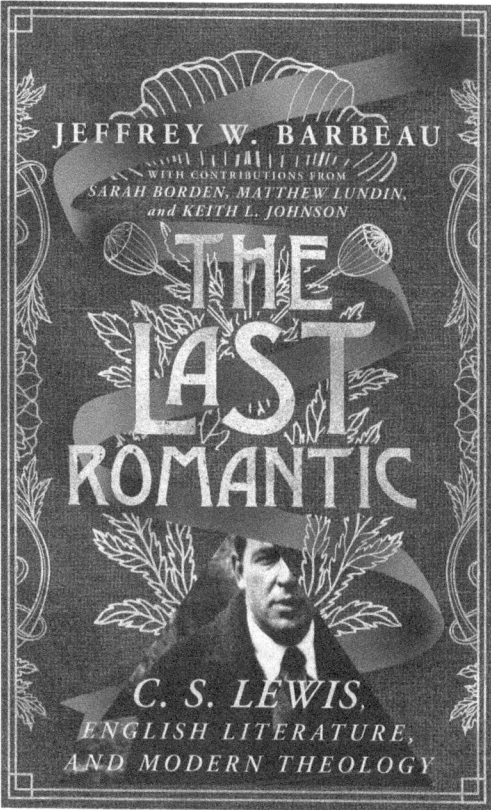

ivp
Academic

An imprint of InterVarsity Press
Downers Grove, Illinois

InterVarsity Press
P.O. Box 1400 | Downers Grove, IL 60515-1426
ivpress.com | email@ivpress.com

InterVarsity Press® is the publishing division of InterVarsity Christian Fellowship/USA®. For more information, visit intervarsity.org.

Scriptures marked KJV are from the King James Version, public domain.

The publisher cannot verify the accuracy or functionality of website URLs used in this book beyond the date of publication.

Cover design: David Fassett
Interior design: Daniel van Loon
Cover image: C. S. Lewis at Stonehenge, April 8, 1925. Photo collection call number: CSL-A / P-5.
        Marion E. Wade Center, Wheaton College, Wheaton, IL. Used by permission.

ISBN 978-1-5140-1051-8 (print) | ISBN 978-1-5140-1052-5 (digital)

Printed in the United States of America ∞

Library of Congress Cataloging-in-Publication Data
Names: Barbeau, Jeffrey W., author.
Title: The last romantic : C.S. Lewis, English literature, and modern
   theology / Jeffrey W. Barbeau.
Description: Downers Grove, IL : IVP Academic, [2025] | Series: Hansen
   lectureship series | Includes bibliographical references and index.
Identifiers: LCCN 2024031173 (print) | LCCN 2024031174 (ebook) | ISBN
   9781514010518 (paperback) | ISBN 9781514010525 (ebook)
Subjects: LCSH: Lewis, C. S. (Clive Staples), 1898-1963–Criticism and
   interpretation. | Romanticism. | Theology in literature. | English
   literature–20th century–History and criticism. | BISAC: RELIGION /
   Christianity / Literature & the Arts | LITERARY CRITICISM / European /
   English, Irish, Scottish, Welsh
Classification: LCC PR6023.E926 Z5847 2025 (print) | LCC PR6023.E926
   (ebook) | DDC 823/.912–dc23/eng/20240819
LC record available at https://lccn.loc.gov/2024031173
LC ebook record available at https://lccn.loc.gov/2024031174

32   31   30   29   28   27   26   25 | 12   11   10   9   8   7   6   5   4   3   2

In memory of

ROGER LUNDIN

Scholar, teacher, friend

CONTENTS

PREFACE
G. Walter Hansen

I WAS DELIGHTED BY DR. JEFFREY BARBEAU'S "C. S. Lewis and the Romantic Imagination" lectures in 2023. His words evoked vivid images, emotionally charged memories: listening to romantic poetry fifty-six years ago, walking around Walden Pond last week. When Dr. Barbeau began the first lecture with the date autumn 1967, he reawakened the longing I felt in 1967 when I sat in Dr. Clyde Kilby's Romantic Literature class at Wheaton College, drinking from the deep wells of Wordsworth and Coleridge. Now here I was, fifty-six years later, in Dr. Barbeau's "C. S. Lewis and the Romantic Imagination" "class," feeling again the power of imagination, the wonder of beauty in nature, and the mystery of divine presence in sacraments.

Dr. Barbeau's extensive reading of the marginalia in the personal library of C. S. Lewis held by the Marion E. Wade Center gives us a fresh understanding of the influence of the Romantic poets on Lewis. Barbeau showed us a poem Lewis wrote on a page at the back of his own copy of *The Shorter Poems of William Wordsworth* (1917), inspired by his beloved mentor. He helps us to see how often Lewis followed the legacy of Romanticism by beginning with subjectivity of the interior life. Yet Lewis argues from personal experience to the universality of objective values. Lewis's "Romantic argument," the way he builds universal, objective moral law (the Tao) from subjective feelings, runs through *The Abolition of Man*.

Another memory from my college experience in 1967 came to my mind when Barbeau said that "the most profound and pressing questions" of Lewis's own life can be seen in his quest to understand the relationship between subjective, personal experience and the knowledge of objective reality. At the same time I took Kilby's class, I was happily lost in Dr. Art Holmes's Epistemology class—and asking the very same questions. I'm still asking those questions. Barbeau took me a quantum leap forward in my pilgrimage to know the Way, the Truth, and the Life in the wonder and mystery that I find in both nature and the sacraments of divine worship.

Lecture two resonated deeply, this time especially with my wife, Darlene. Like Sarah Congdon, she keeps a journal. Unlike Sarah, Darlene's journal is not in the archive of a college library. She does not self-censor her morning pages. She shreds some of them. Then the shreds become painted prayers in her painting of flowers growing out of golden bowls, blooming as answers from heaven.

Dr. Barbeau shows how the autobiographical books of C. S. Lewis draw on the same rich legacy of life writing that inspired the Methodist piety found in *The Journal of Sarah Eliza Congdon*. A marginal note in Lewis's personal copy of *John Wesley's Journal* indicates he finished reading Wesley's journal soon after the death of his wife, Joy. Lewis followed the Methodist tradition of journaling that shaped Romantic England—journaling as a way of tracking the interior work of the Spirit. In turn, his conversion narrative, *Surprised by Joy,* and the story of his mourning, *A Grief Observed*, were shaped by the personal narrative poems of William Wordsworth and Samuel Taylor Coleridge.

Even though Lewis feared that his life story, *Surprised by Joy*, was "suffocatingly subjective,"[1] he charged ahead to tell of his own interior journey from atheism to Christian faith. Barbeau shows us that Lewis alludes to Romanticism not only in the title, a line taken from a poem by Wordsworth, but also by writing "in the same spirit as Wordsworth's *The Prelude*" in his own personal narrative.

---

[1]C. S. Lewis, *Surprised by Joy: The Shape of My Early Life* (Boston: Mariner, 2012), viii.

In lecture three, Barbeau begins with the fascinating story of the origin and making of Lewis's wardrobe, now standing in the Marion E. Wade Center. Barbeau then leads us to consider the role of the symbol in Romanticism as a way of understanding Lewis's view of nature, imagination, and the numinous experience of God. Barbeau's reference to a marginal note by Lewis captured my attention: "I wonder are Melville, Emerson, Nietzche [*sic*], Carlyle & few other in Nineteenth Century rumblings of the great collapse wh. came in our own?" Emerson!? I am surprised by this mention of Emerson. I see Ralph Waldo Emerson's name ubiquitously displayed where I live near Concord, Massachusetts. He's the "sage of Concord," renowned for his wisdom and love of nature. When I take our out-of-town guests for a walk around Walden Pond, we sit in the replica of Thoreau's cabin and stand with other pilgrims at the sacred spot where Thoreau built his cabin on Emerson's land. I give them a copy of *Walden Pond* as well as Emerson's *Nature Poems*. And I tell my friends about the transcendentalists of Concord and what their words have to offer us today.

Why did Lewis say that Emerson was a rumbling of the great collapse? As I listened to Barbeau speak about Lewis's response to the Romantic legacy of nature worship, I kept thinking of Emerson, also an heir of the Romantic legacy. My imagination gave me a "vision in a dream" of Lewis and Emerson walking around Walden Pond. They stand in silence absorbing the beauty of the sunlight, clouds, and forest reflected in the pond. Emerson recounts his pilgrimage in August 1833 to visit Wordsworth and Coleridge in England. He reports in detail his conversation with Coleridge at Highgate, London, and Wordsworth at his home on Rydal Mount.[2] Lewis speaks of reading and rereading Wordsworth's *The Prelude* with increasing pleasure and understanding.

---

[2]Ralph Waldo Emerson, *English Traits*, in *Essays and Lectures* (New York: Library of America, 1983), 770-78.

In my imagined conversation, Emerson tells Lewis that nature leads him to see that "all the currents of the Universal Being circulate through me; I am part or particle of God."[3]

Lewis responds,

> Nature never taught me that there exists a God of glory and infinite majesty. I had to learn that in other ways. But nature gave the word *glory* a meaning for me. I still do not know where else I could have found one. I do not see how the "fear" of God could have ever meant to me anything but the lowest prudential efforts to be safe, if I had never seen certain ominous ravines and unapproachable crags. And if nature had never awakened certain longings in me, huge areas of what I can now mean by the "love of God" would never, so far as I can see, have existed.[4]

As I walk close and listen, I begin to understand why Lewis said that Emerson was a rumbling of a great collapse. In Emerson's rumbling of a great collapse, heaven collapsed into nature, nature collapsed into his spirit. Nature became his God; Emerson became God and Emerson lost God.[5] As Lewis advises us, "We must make a *détour*—leave the hills and woods and go back to our studies, to church, to our Bibles, to our knees. Otherwise the love of nature is beginning to turn into a nature religion. And then, even if it does not lead us to the Dark Gods, it will lead us to a great deal of nonsense."[6] I'd like to walk with Dr. Barbeau around Walden Pond and listen to him imagine a conversation between Lewis and Emerson.

I love the way Barbeau closes lecture three by teaching us with lines of Wordsworth that "nature and imagination draw us into love."

---

[3]Emerson, "Nature," in *Essays and Lectures*, 10.
[4]C. S. Lewis, *The Four Loves* (New York: HarperCollins, 1960), 25-26.
[5]See Roger Lundin, *From Nature to Experience: The American Search for Cultural Authority* (Lanham, MD: Rowman & Littlefield, 2005), 41-70.
[6]Lewis, *Four Loves*, 27.

> From love, for here
> Do we begin and end, all grandeur comes,
> All truth and beauty, from pervading love,
> That gone, we are as dust.[7]

In *Surprised by Joy* and *The Four Loves*, Lewis appeals to human and divine love as the way of knowing truth and beauty. In fact, I think the final lines of Wordsworth's *The Prelude* describe the Romantics: Wordsworth, Lewis, and Barbeau:

> Prophets of Nature, we to them will speak
> A lasting inspiration, sanctified
> By reason and by truth: what we have loved
> Others will love; and we may teach them how—[8]

Thank you, Jeff, for teaching us, in the good company of the Romantics, what you love, and for teaching us how to love with imagination.

THE KEN AND JEAN HANSEN LECTURESHIP

I was motivated to set up a lectureship in honor of my parents, Ken and Jean Hansen, at the Wade Center primarily because they loved Marion E. Wade. My father began working for Mr. Wade in 1946, the year I was born. He launched my father's career and mentored him in business. Often when I look at the picture of Marion Wade in the Wade Center, I give thanks to God for his beneficial influence in my family and in my life.

After Darlene and I were married in December 1967, the middle of my senior year at Wheaton College, we invited Marion and Lil Wade for dinner in our apartment. I wanted Darlene to get to know the best storyteller I've ever heard.

---

[7]William Wordsworth, *The Prelude* (1805), book 13.149-52, in *Wordsworth's Poetry and Prose*, Norton critical ed., ed. Nicholas Halmi (New York: Norton, 2014), 369-70.
[8]Wordsworth, *The Prelude* (1805), book 13.442-45, in *Wordsworth's Poetry and Prose*, 377.

When Marion Wade passed through death into the Lord's presence on November 28, 1973, his last words to my father were, "Remember Joshua, Ken." As Joshua was the one who followed Moses to lead God's people, my father was the one who followed Marion Wade to lead the ServiceMaster Company.

After members of Marion Wade's family and friends at Service-Master set up a memorial fund in honor of Marion Wade at Wheaton College, my parents initiated the renaming of Clyde Kilby's collection of papers and books from the seven British authors—C. S. Lewis, J. R. R. Tolkien, Dorothy L. Sayers, George MacDonald, G. K. Chesterton, Charles Williams, and Owen Barfield—as the Marion E. Wade Collection.

I was also motivated to name this lectureship after my parents because they loved the literature of these seven authors, whose papers are now collected at the Wade Center.

While I was still in college, my father and mother took an evening course on Lewis and Tolkien with Dr. Kilby. The class was limited to nine students so that they could meet in Dr. Kilby's living room. Dr. Kilby's wife, Martha, served tea and cookies.

My parents were avid readers, collectors, and promoters of the books of the seven Wade authors, even hosting a book club in their living room led by Dr. Kilby. When they moved to Santa Barbara in 1977, they named their home Rivendell, after the beautiful house of the elf Lord Elrond, whose home served as a welcome haven to weary travelers as well as a cultural center for Middle-earth history and lore. Family and friends who stayed in their home know that their home fulfilled Tolkien's description of Rivendell:

> And so at last they all came to the Last Homely House, and found its doors flung wide. . . . [The] house was perfect whether you liked food, or sleep, or work, or story-telling, or singing, or just sitting and thinking best, or a pleasant mixture

of them all. . . . Their clothes were mended as well as their bruises, their tempers and their hopes. . . . Their plans were improved with the best advice.[9]

Our family treasures many memories of our times at Rivendell, highlighted by storytelling. Our conversations often drew from images of the stories of Lewis, Tolkien, and the other authors. We had our own code language: "That was a terrible Bridge of Khazad-dûm experience." "That meeting felt like the Council of Elrond."

One cold February, Clyde and Martha Kilby escaped the deep freeze of Wheaton to thaw out and recover for two weeks at my parents' Rivendell home in Santa Barbara. As a thank-you note, Clyde Kilby dedicated his book *Images of Salvation in the Fiction of C. S. Lewis* to my parents. When my parents set up our family foundation in 1985, they named the foundation Rivendell Stewards' Trust.

In many ways, they lived in and lived out the stories of the seven authors. It seemed fitting and proper, therefore, to name this lectureship in honor of Ken and Jean Hansen.

Escape for Prisoners

The purpose of the Hansen Lectureship is to provide a way of escape for prisoners. J. R. R. Tolkien writes about the positive role of escape in literature:

I have claimed that Escape is one of the main functions of fairy-stories, and since I do not disapprove of them, it is plain that I do not accept the tone of scorn or pity with which "Escape" is now so often used: a tone for which the uses of the word outside literary criticism give no warrant at all. In what the misusers of

---

[9]J. R. R. Tolkien, *The Hobbit* (London: Unwin Hyman, 1987), 50-51.

Escape are fond of calling Real Life, Escape is evidently as a rule very practical, and may even be heroic.[10]

Note that Tolkien is not talking about escap*ism* or an avoidance of reality but rather the idea of escape as a means of providing a new view of reality, the true, transcendent reality that is often screened from our view in this fallen world. He adds:

> Evidently we are faced by a misuse of words, and also by a confusion of thought. Why should a man be scorned, if, finding himself in prison, he tries to get out and go home? Or if, when he cannot do so, he thinks and talks about other topics than jailers and prison-walls? The world outside has not become less real because the prisoner cannot see it. In using Escape in this [derogatory] way the [literary] critics have chosen the wrong word, and, what is more, they are confusing, not always by sincere error, the Escape of the Prisoner with the Flight of the Deserter.[11]

I am not proposing that these lectures give us a way to escape from our responsibilities or ignore the needs of the world around us but rather that we explore the stories of the seven authors to escape from a distorted view of reality, from a sense of hopelessness, and to awaken us to the true hope of what God desires for us and promises to do for us.

C. S. Lewis offers a similar vision for the possibility that such literature could open our eyes to a new reality:

> We want to escape the illusions of perspective. . . . We want to see with other eyes, to imagine with other imaginations, to feel with other hearts, as well as with our own. . . .

---

[10]J. R. R. Tolkien, "On Fairy-Stories," in *Tales from the Perilous Realm* (Boston: Houghton Mifflin, 2008), 375.

[11]Tolkien, "On Fairy-Stories," 376.

The man who is contented to be only himself, and therefore less a self, is in prison. My own eyes are not enough for me, I will see through those of others. . . .

In reading great literature I become a thousand men yet remain myself. . . . Here as in worship, in love, in moral action, and in knowing, I transcend myself; and am never more myself than when I do.[12]

The purpose of the Hansen Lectureship is to explore the great literature of the seven Wade authors so that we can escape from the prison of our self-centeredness and narrow, parochial perspective in order to see with other eyes, feel with other hearts, and be equipped for practical deeds in real life.

As a result, we will learn new ways to experience and extend the fulfillment of our Lord's mission: "to proclaim freedom for the prisoners and recovery of sight for the blind, to set the oppressed free" (Lk 4:18 NIV).

---

[12]C. S. Lewis, *An Experiment in Criticism* (Cambridge: Cambridge University Press, 1965), 137, 140-41.

ACKNOWLEDGMENTS

I EXTEND MY APPRECIATION to all who have contributed to the formation and publication of this book. Above all, I owe a great debt to Walter and Darlene Hansen, who have established their lectureship in honor of Walter's parents, Ken and Jean Hansen; I hope to take up their kind invitation to walk Walden Pond alongside them soon! David Downing and Crystal Downing, former co-directors of the Wade, cannot be praised highly enough for their enthusiastic insight and encouragement; since they first came to Wheaton, I have enjoyed watching them flourish in their work and look forward to seeing the fruit of their labor in the years to come. At the Wade, I also benefited from the wisdom and kindness of Marjorie Mead, Laura Stanifer, Jill Walker, Melissa Doogan, and Hope Grant; Marj and Laura have proven especially supportive colleagues throughout this process, with Laura providing exemplary assistance at every stage. The work of the entire staff has so inspired me that I share the riches of the Wade to all who will listen. All materials from the Marion E. Wade Center appear by permission ("Wade"). I am grateful for the support of Heidi Truty, who assembled the index. The team at InterVarsity Press, including Jon Boyd, Rebecca Carhart, and Ellen Hsu, has been a pleasure to work with. Thanks to David Stiver, Lisa Benner, Cyprian Consiglio, and the Bede Griffiths Trust for their support of my inquiries and request for permissions related to Bede Griffiths. My thanks to Rachel Churchill and the C. S. Lewis Company LTD for permission to print selections from C. S. Lewis.

I am humbled by the thoughtful remarks of my three respondents—Sarah Borden, Matthew Lundin, and Keith Johnson—for each has provided me a great deal to reflect on in my reading of Lewis and modernity more generally; I have offered a few brief comments on their responses in my conclusion. Archival and library support at Wheaton College was provided by Katherine Graber, Emily Banas, and Bob Shuster. Sarah Stanley first introduced me to *The Journal of Sarah Congdon*, which has maintained a foothold in my mind ever since. I also owe a debt to Aaron Hill for first sharing with me, many years ago, the *Faculty Bulletin* articles I refer to in the first chapter—all is gift, indeed. Special thanks to Sam Ashton, who engaged in initial archival research at my request and first drew my attention to the possibility of unpublished poems by Lewis in the Wordsworth volume. In addition to two separate classes of students, who each challenged me to think carefully about C. S. Lewis and his times, other colleagues at Wheaton and elsewhere have provided helpful insight and support along the way, including Murray Evans, Richard Gibson, Kristen Page, James Beitler, Tim Larsen, Simon Saleem, David Lauber, Norbert Feinendegen, and Mark Noll. Several members of my family were able to attend the lectures in person; seeing their faces in the crowd buoyed my spirits. Other family members were unable to attend but listened carefully to recordings, asked questions, and provided supportive feedback. To these and all those who heard the lectures, offered warm greetings, or wrote to me afterwards, I thank you very much for your kind interest.

Finally, I have dedicated this book to the memory of Roger Lundin (1949–2015). Years ago, I had the immense pleasure of co-teaching a course on transatlantic Romanticism with him that will long remain one of the most memorable teaching experiences of my career. Roger's dynamism as a lecturer, pastoral care as a mentor, and openhanded friendship have contributed to my life no less than his exemplary model of scholarship in the field of theology and literature.

INTRODUCTION

I THOUGHT FOR A LONG TIME that C. S. Lewis was something of a rationalist. The air of confidence implicit in titles on notoriously knotty subjects such as pain and miracles. The simplistic analysis of Jesus as liar, lunatic, or Lord. The tendency among some to use his works as a foil against an encroaching liberalism, always available with a pithy quote to settle a troublesome controversy.

All this left me a bit uneasy. But what if Lewis wasn't like that caricature at all? As I explain in this book, I had good reason for my apprehension, but it was only after I came back to Lewis's works—after years steeped in modern theology and British Romantic literature, just as Lewis was himself—that I figured out why.

I must admit that I'm still surprised by my journey. One of my earliest encounters with Lewis's writing came when I was only around ten or eleven years old. Someone had given me the Chronicles of Narnia as a gift, so I began reading *The Lion, the Witch, and the Wardrobe*. Soon, I found myself caught in a bind, for I intuited a likeness between Aslan and Jesus. Did this book promote a kind of idolatry? Would I risk spiritual confusion if I continued to read? With no one to guide me, I sold the multivolume series in a garage sale not long after. I still remember the woman who purchased the set asking, "Are you sure you really want to part with these?"

Years later, I rediscovered Lewis as an undergraduate. I devoured his nonfiction prose. Lewis provided a sustenance that I desperately needed in my earliest theological studies. I was a student of historical theology but eager to understand Christianity also in its practical aspect—not as a philosophy or a set of dogmatic formulas but as a way of life. For my senior project, I decided against the typical pattern of biblical and systematic approaches in favor of a study of Lewis that considered theology from a literary perspective. At the defense, one of my faculty readers suggested that my work would be stronger with greater attention to the Bible, but he didn't understand what I was seeking.

Subsequently, I pursued English literature as a graduate student. I was now in the thrall of literary theory; this was a time of exploration, weighing the latest trends in deconstruction, reader-response criticism, and a host of new approaches to literature that opened possibilities I had seldom, if ever, encountered before. I still loved Lewis but largely left him behind, scratching my head at his seeming intractability to the dynamic interpretative questions facing readers in a poststructuralist age.

After further work in theology and religious studies, I began teaching as a university professor. Lewis became something of a prop in my repertoire—an easy reference for students wary or uncertain about a difficult idea. One quip from Lewis and their minds were instantaneously put at ease. Though I often relied on him implicitly, I had forgotten that I had been nursed by Lewis's ideas in my earliest theological formation.

Only when I was invited to prepare a series of lectures for the Marion E. Wade Center did I begin to remember that many of my own best insights stemmed from Lewis's writings. (In 2023 I delivered these lectures, titled "C. S. Lewis and the Romantic Imagination," as part of the Ken and Jean Hansen Lectureship series. This book is based on those addresses.) The ebullient directors of the Wade, David and Crystal Downing, had asked me to consider the relationship between C. S. Lewis and British Romanticism, a topic to which I have devoted much of my professional career. I had spent more than two decades thinking about the relationship between Romantic literature and its religious context in Britain but never imagined I'd find more than a series of interesting observations on several beloved poems or a few barbed comments on the alleged irreligion of these authors.

I could not have been more wrong.

In my first foray into the subject, I taught a class on C. S. Lewis and modern theology. I blanched when, on our first evening together, I learned that many of my most eager students appeared to know Lewis's works better than I did! I owe much to them, for while some already had a thoroughgoing grasp of the major plot points, characters, and themes, they cheerfully pressed on through our rigorous schedule, as we paired each new book with major theologians for discussion throughout the semester. We read through the bulk of Lewis's works together, and I found myself rereading almost every book we studied multiple times as I sought a greater grasp of Lewis in his intellectual context.

Next, I threw myself into the archives of the Wade. I began by reading what others had said about Lewis and Romanticism. The results were mixed and not especially promising. I already had an inkling of what I wanted to say about Lewis, but I worried that he could sometimes mention a name or idea with little or no indication of his purpose. I still required the sorts of connections that I knew from experience only time spent in an archive can produce.

What I discovered was nothing short of a revelation. At first, I was dismayed that Lewis's personal library often lacked the sort of expansive marginalia that I have come to cherish in some other writers I've written about. Over time, however, I came to recognize in Lewis's careful notations and markings an untold key to his own reading habits. More than once as I sat in the quiet of the Wade, I found myself nearly shouting out loud, "I've found it!" in response to a new link or association.

My admiration for Lewis expanded in the process. Before, I'd regarded him as something of a theological dilettante—a view I've come to recognize as the product of his own rather slippery rhetoric—ever warning readers that he is little more than an amateur. Now, for the first time, I could demonstrate his careful reading habits with concrete evidence. Lewis read the Greats at Oxford and continued to study the history of philosophy, theology, and literature throughout his life, demonstrating in unpublished marginalia a command of modern thought that I had little appreciation for in reading his popular works alone.

Often, I would find in Lewis's library a correction or comment that cross-referenced a single sentence—one that I might easily overlook, sometimes hundreds of pages apart—in which an author had contradicted some earlier assertion. Elsewhere, Lewis would track with a dense philosophical treatise in summary paraphrases at the top or bottom of the page, indicating his attentiveness to the volume at hand. I could almost picture him sitting in a chair with this very book before him!

There are hundreds—nay, thousands—of such books in the Wade archive. To be sure, I did not examine marginalia in every volume of Lewis's personal library in preparing my lectures, but I did work painstakingly through an extraordinary range of his library in works related to eighteenth-, nineteenth-, and twentieth-century literature, as well as many of his theological and philosophical tomes from these and other periods. As a result, I came to see that Lewis was not only *familiar* with the questions of his own age but also *reflecting* and even *responding* to many of the same issues in his most well-known prose.

Three pivotal ideas emerged through this meticulous, systematic process. First, Lewis often approached some of the most challenging questions of Christian thought through the lens of the personal. Far from offering readers dogmatic assertions about faith, Lewis often begins with experience, intuition, and religious feeling. This certainly reflects both the British Romantic movement, which I found him citing at every turn, and the spirit of his own times. In the first chapter, I take up this idea, showing that Lewis not only relies on the British Romantics far more than many might expect (given his scholarly reputation in medieval and Renaissance literature), but he also writes with an awareness of the legacy of modern philosophy and the so-called subjective turn that shaped much of the nineteenth and twentieth centuries.

Second, Lewis enjoyed an uneasy relationship with spiritual autobiography and what scholars today call, more broadly, "life writing." While he complained that his own efforts in the genre were "suffocatingly subjective," Lewis appeals to the great tradition of conversion narratives and other forms of autobiographical writing to introduce Christian thought to a wide audience. In this, Lewis reflects many of his Anglican forebears, including the Methodists John and Charles Wesley, as well as the life writings of British Romantic poets such as William Wordsworth. In fact, as I explain in the second chapter, just as Lewis was deliberating theism (and Christianity) as a viable option for his own life, he was also reading deeply in the philosophical theology of Romantic poets such as Samuel Taylor Coleridge.

Third, I was struck repeatedly while reading Lewis's works just how often he discusses the natural world. His fiction often shows an acute interest in the description of landscapes, and in nonfiction works he makes reference to a love for nature that, at the very least, raises decidedly modern questions about how an appreciation for beauty relates to our knowledge of God. In such a light, as I show in the third chapter, Lewis's repetition of British Romantic ideas of imagination, visionary dream states, and symbols stands out as major features in his works. Indeed, by bringing Lewis into conversation with the British Romantics, the theological motivation behind his commitment to narrative—to the transformative power of story itself—begins to make sense.

Notably, my research into Lewis's personal library uncovered an exciting new find: previously unpublished poetry by C. S. Lewis that he inscribed in the blank pages at the back of his personal copy of *The Shorter Poems of William Wordsworth* (1917). I have transcribed these poems and included them in the appendix for readers to enjoy, demonstrating in some small way how Lewis's reading in one of the greatest English poets inspired his own poetics. I am grateful to the C. S. Lewis Company and the directors of the Marion E. Wade Center for their permission to publish these for the first time.

One

C. S. LEWIS AND THE "ROMANTIC HERESY"

THE TRIAL OF C. S. LEWIS

Autumn 1967. Several members of Wheaton College entered a lively debate about art, imagination, and Christianity. Parts of their discussion appeared in at least three outlets: a faculty workshop, the *Wheaton Alumni Magazine*, and the *Faculty Bulletin*. Among the contributors to this debate were several prominent faculty members, including philosopher Arthur Holmes, Bible and theology professor Morris Inch, and, initiating the whole discussion, literary critic Clyde S. Kilby.

Only two years earlier, Professor Kilby had successfully petitioned the Wheaton College Library to form a new collection in its holdings. During the prior decade, Kilby had maintained correspondence with the chair of medieval and Renaissance literature at Cambridge, whose popular reputation as an apologist and author of several works of fiction had brought him international acclaim. With the establishment of a formal library collection, Kilby was well on his way to the formation of what we now know as the Marion E. Wade Center. So few will be surprised that Kilby's colleagues associated his thoughts about art and imagination with his overseas interlocutor: C. S. Lewis.

Kilby's remarks, delivered as he looked back on more than thirty years of teaching at the college, appeared in the *Faculty Bulletin* under the provocative title, "The Aesthetic Poverty of Evangelicalism." The essay focuses squarely on what he deems a lack of imagination among Christians in matters of faith. An "evangelical skittishness toward imagination" led to impoverished readings of the Bible and a lack of creativity in the arts. Instead of symbols, figures, and parables, preachers offer little more than strange and negative moral statements that diminish the power of narrative to transform lives.

Fresh attention to aesthetics brought the possibility of renewal. Through the power of imagination, sterile faith might be exchanged for a vibrant awareness of divine mystery, for only such a path could avoid the tendency to fall into cliché, and only such a faculty can give us "the power to see" and express God's glorious ineffability.[1] A renewed vision of aesthetics, Kilby thought, wasn't the safe choice. It was the right one: "You can no more remove the danger from Christianity than you can remove the danger from water, food, light, and love."[2]

While Kilby's essay refers to many significant literary figures—John Milton, Robert Frost, John Donne, among others—there is no mention of Lewis at all. Yet many of Kilby's peers seemed to detect the influence of Lewis behind it all, so it is no exaggeration to suggest that his indictment was understood by many as simultaneously a defense of Lewis. In fact, Kilby's initial paper drew multiple responses in what might be described as a tribunal focused on Lewis's reputation as an orthodox exponent of Christian doctrine.

---

[1] Clyde S. Kilby, "The Aesthetic Poverty of Evangelicalism," *Faculty Bulletin* 31, no. 1 (1967): 9.
[2] Kilby, "Aesthetic Poverty," 6.

"The trial of C. S. Lewis" can hardly be imagined today. As Mark Noll (my immediate predecessor in the Ken and Jean Hansen Lectureship series) has already explained, C. S. Lewis's earliest reception among North American Christians was mixed, but after a tepid response in some circles, his readership steadily expanded among not only Roman Catholics but also Protestants generally. Nevertheless, one can be forgiven for thinking that members of Wheaton College surely had never suffered *any* doubts about Lewis at all—and certainly not in the years immediately after his death—but this is simply not the case. In fact, the most damning charge against Lewis at Wheaton in the 1960s focused on his relationship to the subject of this book. For Lewis was branded a proponent of none other than "the Romantic trend in religion" that some thought had imperiled the historic Christian faith.

Figure 1.1. Morris Inch, Arthur Holmes, and Clyde S. Kilby

The originator of this startling charge against Lewis came in an essay by a Bible and apologetics professor at the college named Morris Inch.[3] While in his essay Professor Inch compliments Kilby for his "outstanding contribution" to the community, he also explains that

---

[3]From the fall 1969 semester, Inch began serving as chair of the Bible Department at Wheaton College.

Kilby's attention to religious epistemology is marked by an acquies-
cence to a dangerous and outmoded vision of God and humanity
alike: "Dr. Kilby rightly warns us against Bibliolatry—the worship of
the letter, but seems to leave us vulnerable to idolatry—worship of the
profane. His demand for artistic sensitivity needs to be heard and
implemented, but the implied flight into an emotive limbo must be
contested, if not in the name of Christianity, at least in that of sanity."[4]

What was the heart of Morris Inch's concern? He feared that
Clyde Kilby risked a misguided, dangerous Romantic epistemology—
in his view, a theory of human knowing that replaced objective fact
with subjective feeling. Inch describes the Romantic movement at
some length, calling it "more of a mood than a creed, a rejection of
the classical norms in literature and art, and an attack on eighteenth-century rationalism. It pled for a return to the natural instincts, to individual predilection, and to creative spontaneity. It
looked at life through the eyes of wonder, and glorified the mystery
of nature."[5]

If Inch's definition seems rather innocuous to our ears today, his
readers surely perceived the objectionable tenor of his claim, for he
proceeded to explain that none other than Friedrich Schleiermacher was the "great champion" of Romanticism. In Schleiermacher,
the Christian faith had succumbed to a damaging liberalism that
threatened true doctrine. Romantics valued emotion rather than
reason, navel-gazing introspection over submission to objective
facts, and immanence instead of transcendence.

By associating Kilby with Schleiermacher, Inch had already
muddied the waters. This was midcentury Wheaton, where

---

[4]Morris Inch, "Shades of Schleiermacher?," *Faculty Bulletin* 31, no. 1 (1967): 32.
[5]Inch, "Shades of Schleiermacher?," 29. Inch's definition brings to mind two recent works:
Kristen Page, *The Wonders of Creation: Learning Stewardship from Narnia and Middle-
Earth*, Hansen Lectureship Series (Downers Grove, IL: IVP Academic, 2022), and
Jeffrey W. Barbeau and Emily Hunter McGowin, eds., *God and Wonder: Theology, Imagi-
nation, and the Arts* (Eugene, OR: Cascade, 2022).

evangelicals were in the process of distinguishing themselves from the fundamentalist culture wars through the likes of *Christianity Today* and Billy Graham. Inch acknowledged as much, recognizing that contemporary evangelicalism was heir to both the "heroic stand for Christian orthodoxy" that those fundamentalist leaders assumed and the "cultural neurosis which developed in its wake."[6]

Professor Inch knew that he was already making an unwelcome claim in associating Kilby's views with the father of modern liberal theology, but instead of stepping delicately around the insinuation, Inch doubled down: "A more recent illustration of the Romantic trend in religion is that of C. S. Lewis."[7] At this point, Inch makes clear that he is fully aware of the gravity of his charge. He has thrown down the gauntlet, implicating both Kilby and Lewis with Schleiermacher. Then, Inch cautiously proceeds: "Some will be horrified to hear me mention Lewis in the same breath with the 'father of modern theological liberalism.'" This was indeed a damning charge, but, having come so far, he would not be dissuaded. "I do," he declares, "and for good reason." For Inch, while Lewis affirms orthodox Christian doctrine, his methodology and epistemology share the defective traits of Schleiermacher's Romanticism. Inch's final judgment is catastrophic: Lewis was a great apologist, but his understanding of biblical authority, theological anthropology, and doctrine of God are all utterly calamitous.

One year later, the *Faculty Bulletin* published a detailed rejoinder to Inch's critique of Kilby. The article, titled "The Romantic Heresy," was written by J. Randall Springer, a graduate student who was soon to complete a master's thesis on C. S. Lewis at the college.[8] From the outset, Springer admits that while his essay focuses on

---

[6]Inch, "Shades of Schleiermacher?," 27.

[7]Inch, "Shades of Schleiermacher?," 29.

[8]J. Randall Springer, "'Beyond Personality': C. S. Lewis' Concept of God" (Wheaton, IL: MA thesis, 1969). Springer later completed a PhD in philosophy at Southern Illinois University, Carbondale (1972) before teaching as a faculty member at Westmont College.

Lewis, he regards his contribution to the debate equally as a defense and "vindication" of Kilby.[9] Springer maintains that most of Inch's charges against Lewis are misguided. At the heart of Springer's argument is a subtle distinction between objective truth and the creative means whereby an individual might express such ideas. Springer writes, "Nothing could be further from Lewis's mind than the Subjectivism of Schleiermacher," for "Man's values must be derived ultimately not from within himself, his own 'experience' or 'feeling,' but from without."[10] Lewis, in Springer's account, is a rationalist, his epistemology is orthodox, and any sign of Romanticism in his writing is little more than "a reaction against the positivism and scientism which we all equally repudiate."[11]

I suspect that Kilby, Inch, and Springer each recognized something in Lewis that remains relevant to understanding his works today. What is the role of what might be called the "subjective" in the thought of C. S. Lewis? While many of Lewis's readers favor his emphasis on the "objective" or rational aspect of his works, I think Professor Inch's critique is not so easily dismissed, even if I don't entirely agree with either his unmitigated condemnation of Romanticism or Springer's naming this tradition the "Romantic heresy."

I think many readers intuit in Lewis's writings something they cannot quite identify—an instinct about Lewis and the ways he appeals to conscience, feelings, and the interior life that asks us to reexamine the role of the subjective in his religious epistemology. Such an emphasis appears throughout many of Lewis's works, but in this chapter I will focus on two of his most beloved nonfiction compositions: *Mere Christianity* and *The Abolition of Man*. My investigation will necessarily take us back to Schleiermacher and the German Romantics, but I will devote far more of my attention to

---

[9]J. Randall Springer, "The Romantic Heresy," *Faculty Bulletin* 31, no. 2 (1968): 18.
[10]Springer, "Romantic Heresy," 20.
[11]Springer, "Romantic Heresy," 22.

the British Romantics that Lewis studied with unceasing interest over the course of his entire life. Through an examination of Lewis's works and his engagement with modern thought, we might begin to see just how significant the influence of Romanticism was for Lewis's life and writings.

THE LAW OF HUMAN NATURE

Perhaps Morris Inch had *Mere Christianity* in mind when he made his disquieting charge. Among the most well-known books in English in the twentieth century, first published as a single text in 1952, *Mere Christianity* began as a series of radio talks between 1942 and 1945. Yet this renowned work displays precisely the sort of emotive rhetoric that leads some to ponder Lewis's method.

Notice the opening line of his opening talk: "Every one has heard people quarrelling."[12] Lewis begins in a rather strange place for a series of lectures on "Right and Wrong as a Clue to the Meaning of the Universe." The chapter, titled "The Law of Human Nature," resonates with readers because Lewis begins precisely with that which some of Lewis's contemporaries would rather he exclude, namely, individual human experience. Instead of identifying a philosophical principle of the good or the true, Lewis starts with the familiar occurrence of arguing with another person. Not only has everyone heard others engaged in such verbal bouts, but everyone also has participated in just such brawls. "It's my turn, not yours!" "You wouldn't like it if I broke your favorite mug!" "Didn't we agree to clean this up together?"

Lewis's purpose in drawing his readers' attention to such language is to demonstrate the existence of a law that is shared by all people, in all places, at all times. Lewis's moral canon works precisely because it is not only known by all *intellectually* but also felt

---

[12]C. S. Lewis, *Mere Christianity* (New York: HarperOne, 2000), 1.

by all *personally*. His examples thereby serve as reminders of a connection between what we sometimes call the subjective and objective. Note well: Lewis does not begin with the affirmation of a knowledge taught only in the Scriptures and available to a few but with an appeal to a universal experience of individual morality (whatever exceptions might be found in the population as a whole).

Notice, too, that Lewis makes clear that the law of human nature is not the same as something so unswerving and unalterable as the law of gravitation.[13] This is neither a fact of nature—such that humans must always and necessarily behave in a particular manner—nor some inventive fancy. Human nature is the result of neither intellection nor appetite. The law of right and wrong results from some third aspect that dictates human behavior: "a moral law, which they did not make, and cannot quite forget even when they try."[14]

Lewis later identifies this sense of the moral law as *conscience*. For Lewis, the notion implies both a consciousness of *something* within human nature and a *someone* "inside ourselves as an influence or a command trying to get us to behave in a certain way."[15] Here, at the crossroads of a law we feel compelled to meet and a mind behind that law we know we ought to obey, Lewis grounds his case for the personal God described by Christianity.

The question I wish to ask is why Lewis begins his case for Christianity with an appeal to personal experience. And I think an additional question that might be posed is why his defense of Christianity was so successful among his listeners and readers. The answer to these questions, I suspect, lies in several different but related movements within modern thought—movements that I think Lewis was more aware of than some scholars admit.

[13]Lewis, *Mere Christianity*, 20.
[14]Lewis, *Mere Christianity*, 23.
[15]Lewis, *Mere Christianity*, 24.

First, I ought to clear up a bugbear that has plagued Lewis's reputation for decades. How many times have I heard it said that Lewis
was *not* a theologian? In truth, I myself have said it more than once.
Yet, as I began to prepare for my lectures on "C. S. Lewis and the
Romantic Imagination," after many years away from his works, I
found myself startled by just how attuned he seems to be to both
ancient and modern theological and philosophical discourse. As I
began to read his unpublished marginalia—carefully examining inscriptions appearing in many of the twenty-five hundred books in
his personal library held by the Marion E. Wade Center—I realized
that Lewis's knowledge of theology and philosophy exceeded what
most readers imagine. Lewis was no mere dilettante, however often
he protested the suggestion that he was an expert in such matters.

In fact, I think we ought to be wary of trusting Lewis's bald-faced
statements about his own inexpertness too much. To adapt an old
adage of writing: distrust what Lewis *tells* you; believe what he
shows you. As we will see at several points in these chapters, Lewis's
tendency to self-deprecation is a rhetorical technique that allows
an Oxford scholar to appear as something of an everyman. He can
tell us that he writes and speaks as an amateur, but the record of his
reading and his delicate handling of complex theological and philosophical concepts often *shows* a different reality. One need only
examine Lewis's careful notation of Baruch Spinoza's *Ethics* in Latin
or his close reading of Immanuel Kant's *Critique of Practical Reason*
to recognize that he was not, strictly speaking, an amateur.

Lewis's literary gift is the remarkable ability to take compli-
cated ideas and make them accessible to a wide audience. This
explains quite a lot, for Lewis knew the needs of his audience and
wrote with an acute sense of how people really think. In the lectures that make up *Mere Christianity*, Lewis offers a defense of
Anglican theology that speaks to a people shellshocked by the
advent of war—a war he knew well and personally suffered from

only two decades earlier. This twin awareness—of the intellectual traditions of the times and the existential crisis of the moment—made Lewis peculiarly equipped for the task he assumes in *Mere Christianity*.

A TASTE FOR THE INFINITE

To understand why reference to Schleiermacher and the tradition that follows him worried Inch, a bit of background may be helpful. For the theologian, Lewis's apologetic gambit in favor of subjectivity makes perfect sense in light of eighteenth- and nineteenth-century German philosophy and theology. While Lewis was not an authority, he was proficient enough to understand recent shifts in the literature. During the prior century, Friedrich Schleiermacher had offered one of the most influential defenses of Christianity in the modern world. In *On Religion: Speeches to Its Cultured Despisers* (1799), Schleiermacher addressed a population increasingly wary of Christianity and religious truth claims generally. Raised in the home of a Prussian military chaplain and trained in Moravian schools before attending the pietist University of Halle, Schleiermacher defended the Christian faith as something far more personal than either right doctrine or ethics alone.

Decisively, in a sign of the times, Schleiermacher addressed his listeners in the language of broad religious need, describing "true religion" as a

Figure 1.2. Friedrich Schleiermacher

"sense and taste for the infinite."[16] In a move against what he perceived around him—a growing tendency toward a cold, rationalist faith—Schleiermacher thought the essence of all religious life was not intellectual attainment or strictly moral action but something deep-seated within the human heart. Religious faith, he explains, "wishes to intuit the universe, wishes devoutly to overthrow the universe's own manifestations and actions, longs to be grasped and filled by the universe's immediate influences in childlike passivity."[17]

In his monumental *The Christian Faith*, Schleiermacher describes this as "the feeling of absolute dependence" that points the individual to God.[18] This means that religious feeling, far from being an unreliable source of knowledge, is at the heart of human understanding of the divine. Religious intuition reflects the "influence of the intuited on the one who intuits."[19] In this, subjectivity points not to subjectivism but to the universal experience of sin and, consequently, the need for redemption.

In fact, though not identical, Schleiermacher and Lewis each make an argument that depends on the notion that something identifiable is happening *within* us that draws us into a knowledge of the God who is also *beyond* us. Schleiermacher describes this as a process in which the finite consciousness becomes aware of "the intuited one" in the universe. Lewis names this as a someone "inside ourselves" who tries to get us to recognize that which lies outside us. So, in a very powerful way, Lewis is admitting that part of what might convince someone to believe in God is the strange feeling that we all have a need for something beyond ourselves.[20]

---

[16] F. D. E. Schleiermacher, *On Religion: Speeches to Its Cultured Despisers*, trans. and ed. Richard Crouter, Cambridge Texts in the History of Philosophy (Cambridge: Cambridge University Press, 1996), 23.

[17] Schleiermacher, *On Religion*, 23.

[18] F. D. E. Schleiermacher, *The Christian Faith* (Edinburgh: T&T Clark, 1989), 26.

[19] Schleiermacher, *On Religion*, 24.

[20] On Schleiermacher, see also Lewis's marginalia in his personal copy of Rudolf Otto, *Religious Essays: A Supplement to "The Idea of the Holy,"* trans. Brian Lunn (London:

Schleiermacher's influential theological vision shaped modern Christian thought throughout the nineteenth century, but he shared his dominion with an intellectual giant who was also one of his colleagues at the University of Berlin. Georg Wilhelm Friedrich Hegel rejected Schleiermacher's approach to religion as a "feeling of absolute dependence," calling the *Speeches* a "virtuoso of edification and enthusiasm."[21] The wording of Hegel's critique is telling. Unlike Schleiermacher, Hegel found such an emphasis on feeling and consciousness destabilizing and self-alienating: "There is nothing that cannot be felt and is not felt. God, truth, and duty are felt, as are evil, falsehood, and wrong. All human states and relationships are felt; all representations of one's own relationship to spiritual and natural things become feelings."[22]

For Hegel, ideas about God and freedom are an objective content that do not depend on

Figure 1.3. Georg Wilhelm Friedrich Hegel

the whimsy of individual opinion. Instead, Hegel theorized a new consciousness of the Absolute that emerges in that which the incarnation of Jesus Christ represents, namely, the manifestation of God in the world.[23] Hegel's

---

Oxford University Press, 1931), 72 and verso of rear free endpaper (C. S. Lewis Library collection, Marion E. Wade Center, Wheaton College, Wheaton, IL. Hereafter, "Wade." © copyright CS Lewis Pte Ltd. Used by permission).

[21]Quoted in James C. Livingston, *Modern Christian Thought: The Enlightenment and the Nineteenth Century*, 2nd ed. (Upper Saddle River, NJ: Prentice Hall, 1997), 1:117.

[22]G. W. F. Hegel, "Foreword to Hinrich's *Religion* (1822)," in *G. W. F. Hegel: Theologian of the Spirit*, ed. Peter C. Hodgson (Minneapolis: Fortress, 1997), 166-67.

[23]On Hegel's concept of Christianity, see Livingston, *Modern Christian Thought*, 1:117-27.

idealism translates Christian doctrine into strikingly philosophical terms, leaving the concrete historical events of the incarnation in a position of only secondary importance. For Hegel, Christianity thereby articulates the real goal of history as the union of finite and infinite. Such a union occurs in the current age as individuals engage in acts of self-abdication, surrendering to the kingdom of the Spirit.

Lewis knew the challenge of even understanding Hegel: he once compared his own incapacity to lecture during severe illness to "a Lecture on Hegel from a drunk man."[24] Yet, more seriously, Lewis feared that Hegel's thought led only to a pantheistic identification between God and the world. This, he believed, was the state of mind most people would slip into on their own. In religion, Lewis believed such a view shared more with Hinduism than Christianity, since the latter is the only significant alternative to pantheism.[25] But when pressed on the matter, Lewis admitted to one correspondent that his own views were likely shaped as much if not more by Hegel's interpreters than by the writings of the man, since few interpreters seemed to agree on Hegel's real meaning.[26]

In fact, the most incisive developments to the problem of conscience after Schleiermacher and Hegel appear in what has become known as "left-wing Hegelianism." Although several philosophers and theologians belong to this tradition, including demythologist David Friedrich Strauss, one of the most fateful developments of Hegelian philosophy appears in the writings of his erstwhile student at Berlin, Ludwig Feuerbach. The varied conceptions of self-consciousness that Schleiermacher and Hegel each theorized in defense of Christian faith become in Feuerbach the basis of one of modern theology's severest critiques.

---

[24]C. S. Lewis, *The Collected Letters of C. S. Lewis*, ed. Walter Hooper (New York: Harper-Collins, 2004-2007), 3:1442 (July 15, 1963); hereafter *CLCSL*.

[25]C. S. Lewis, *Miracles: A Preliminary Study* (New York: HarperCollins, 2000), 132.

[26]*CLCSL* 3:1388 (December 8, 1962).

In his landmark publication, *The Essence of Christianity* (1841), Feuerbach maintained that Hegel's vindication of Christianity (even in starkly modern terms) falls short since any discussion of human consciousness of an "other" points not to the existence of God but only to the existence of the self: "In the object which he contemplates, therefore, man becomes acquainted with himself; consciousness of the objective is the self-consciousness of man."[27] Such a shift also implicates Schleiermacher: the feeling of the Absolute really amounts to little more than the projection of the self as other. Consciousness is not the perception of God or Absolute Spirit but only the "I" supposed as a "thou." Faith, in such a view, is little more than a function of human psychology.

Feuerbach's materialism was the most devastating critique of Christianity since David Hume's naturalist empiricism. For some, such a projection of the self makes suspect all religious truth claims as little more than illusory wish-fulfillment (as for Sigmund Freud). Alternately, the self as other only provides a means of coping with economic and political alienation (as for Karl Marx). Lewis rejected these ideas as inadequate and misleading, for they fail to take account of how Christian doctrine and practice often run counter to self-interest.

Still, one might reasonably ask whether Lewis really had nineteenth-century theology and philosophy in view—from

Figure 1.4. Sigmund Freud

---

[27]Ludwig Feuerbach, *The Essence of Christianity*, trans. George Eliot (Amhurst, NY: Prometheus, 1989), 5.

Schleiermacher to left-wing Hegelianism—when he opened his lectures in *Mere Christianity*. As even a few examples can easily illustrate, such an appeal to self-consciousness and moral experience is certainly not foreign to the Christian tradition. Augustine's opening meditation in the *Confessions* involves a deep sense of self-knowledge that leads him from restlessness in sin to peace in God. Later, Anselm's ontolog-

Figure 1.5. Karl Marx

ical argument for the existence of God depended on the supposition of the divine as the realization of the highest conception of being. Even John Calvin's *Institutes* looks to the interior self, beginning with the inward-looking gaze that shifts abruptly from the self to God when faced with the reality of sin. Certainly, Lewis's appeal to self-consciousness and the interior life belongs to a longer tradition of reflection on the relationship between knowledge of God and the self.

I must admit that, for some time, I was unsure about Lewis's intellectual debts in his appeal to individual conscience in *Mere Christianity* and elsewhere. I had no doubt that Lewis was aware of modern philosophy, but I remained skeptical. Then I discovered a book in C. S. Lewis's own library that corroborates what I had never previously been able to confirm. In his copy of Friedrich von Hügel's *Essays & Addresses on the Philosophy of Religion* (1928), Lewis notes a history of nineteenth-century materialism that verifies his familiarity with this intellectual history. Breaking with his frequent practice of limiting handwritten notes to direct underlining, marginal lines, or summary comments, Lewis's personal copy includes a detailed sketch of the nineteenth-century Hegelian tradition.

In the chapter "Religion and Illusion," von Hügel makes a statement that Lewis identifies as potentially confusing, claiming that the subject requires attention to none other than Ludwig Feuerbach: "I want to take the problem, not according to any formulation of my own, but in the combination of remarkable psychological penetration, of rare knowledge throughout large reaches of the religious consciousness, and of sceptical assumptions and passion presented by Ludwig Feuerbach, in by far his greatest work, *Das Wesen des Christenthums*."[28] At this point in the text, Lewis adds his own footnote, directing the reader to weigh this statement carefully: "To the English reader this seems a very odd person to select as a representative."[29] He then points readers to a later page in the same book.

Turning to the later passage, the reader discovers a precis in Lewis's own handwriting at the close of a chapter "Progress in Religion" (figure 1.6). Referring back to the prior page, Lewis traces the intellectual history of Hegelianism with specific attention to Feuerbach: "Feuerbach is selected because the author regards the real power of scepticism as resting not with the naïf materialists but with the 'Hegelians of the Left.'" He then highlights a series of steps, beginning with an explanation of two schools of thought: "Hegel's absolutism can be read either in such an immanentist sense that the Absolute means little more than 'the empirical world coherently described,' or in such a transcendental sense that it is almost identical with God." The immediate response to Hegel, Lewis claims, was an "atheistical reading" that brought about a philosophy of religious idealism in two camps. Right-wing Hegelianism "rightly understood

---

[28]Friedrich von Hügel, *Essays & Addresses on the Philosophy of Religion* (London: J. M. Dent & Sons, 1928), 29.

[29]Marginalia by C. S. Lewis in von Hügel, *Essays & Addresses*, 29 (C. S. Lewis Library collection, Wade).

agrees with Christianity."[30] The left wing includes Strauss, who relied on myth to bypass debates about Scriptures as "fact or lie," and Feuerbach, who claimed, "All theology is psychology" and "the wish is the fundamental phenomenon in religion." Lewis continues, briskly summarizing his understanding of Feuerbach's thought: "God is a projection of what we most value in ourselves: therefore at first necessary in order that we may come to know our own nature: but easily becomes dangerous. The right course is to to [*sic*] continue to reverence the qualities we have given this 'projected' God while getting rid of the projection." Lewis concludes his exercise with a final stage in the history: "Marx. Full materialism."[31]

These previously unpublished marginalia provide insight into what may be driving Lewis's rhetoric in books such as *Mere Christianity*. While his published works include only passing reference to German philosophers such as Hegel, his private marginalia indicate a keen attentiveness to recent developments in continental philosophy and theology—developments that had made a public defense of Christianity peculiarly challenging in the middle of the twentieth century. Feuerbach was still

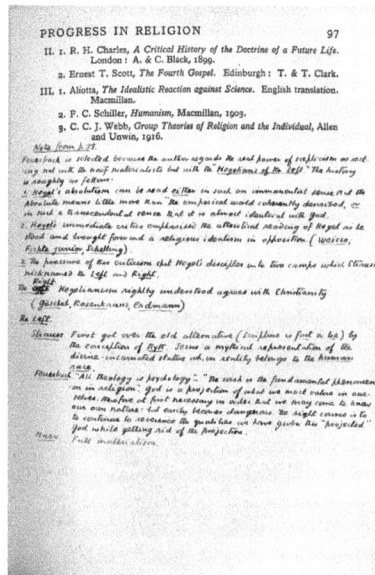

Figure 1.6. Marginalia by C. S. Lewis in Friedrich von Hügel, *Essays & Addresses on the Philosophy of Religion*

---

[30]Here, Lewis specifically mentions the work of Karl Friedrich Göschel (1784–1861), Karl Rosenkranz (1805–1879), and Johann Eduard Erdmann (1805–1892).

[31]Marginalia by C. S. Lewis, in von Hügel, *Essays & Addresses*, 97 (C. S. Lewis Library collection, Wade).

relatively unknown among many English readers, but for the
Christian apologist his work on subjectivity shapes the possibilities
and limits of arguments from conscience.

ALONE IN THE DESERT

When Lewis begins *Mere Christianity* with an appeal to the law of
right and wrong, he does so because he recognizes something
about his audience that we might overlook. Part of this harks back
to the thorny nineteenth-century debates about subjectivity and
objectivity that I have just traced. However, the German philosophical tradition is only part of the story. Lewis knows that his
listeners will find the argument from morality convincing because
he knows that arguments from personal experience are also powerful in the English theological tradition.

Understanding this background may clarify what appears to be
a contradiction in terms at the commencement of the fourth
section of *Mere Christianity*: "Beyond Personality: or First Steps in
the Doctrine of the Trinity." In what I regard as among the most
compelling passages in the entire work, Lewis compares Christianity to a map of the ocean, offering a remarkable explanation
about the relationship between personal experience and the truths
of faith. Here, Lewis cautions against the error of subjectivity, even
as he affirms religious experience as profoundly meaningful.[32]

The passage begins with one of those characteristic remarks that
Lewis uses to redirect his readers. He shrewdly suggests that some
think he ought not tell them about theology—but he will do it
anyway. Instead of treating his readers as children, he will give
them the mature insights that he believes they really desire. This is
Lewis at his best: disarming readers by reminding them that they
are too sophisticated to follow their own, baser instincts.

---

[32]Consider Kathleen Norris's description of *Mere Christianity* as a book that advances not
a philosophy but a life, alluding to a similar remark in Coleridge's *Aids to Reflection*
(1825). (See the foreword in *Mere Christianity*, xix.)

Lewis then tells the story of the hard-bitten officer.[33] A member of the Royal Air Force, the man interrupts Lewis—seemingly mid-sentence during a lecture at an otherwise staid event—to say that any talk of theology is a distraction from a genuine, personal experience of God. He doesn't require dogma or doctrine. He's felt God himself "out alone in the desert at night: the tremendous mystery."[34] This man claims to know a truth that many in the church seem to ignore. Christian doctrine is stale and rigid when compared to the real thing. Creeds and formularies make an organized religion, but the one who really knows God recognizes all that as little more than a pale imitation. Theology is forgery. Counterfeit beliefs stand in the place of enigmatic power.

Disarming his readers yet again, Lewis immediately affirms the hard-bitten officer's experience. His was indeed a real, experiential knowledge of God compared to which formulaic statements of historic Christianity offer little more than insipid impersonation. But—and here's the rub—Lewis thinks something similar is in play when an individual turns from the experience of swimming in the ocean to a map of an ocean designed for maritime navigation. Suddenly the cool water, splashing waves, and salt-filled air are nullified in solid lines and static colors that diminish the effervescence of the real thing. Unlike our experiences of the seas, however, maps collate many different perspectives, fitting them in a single, accessible portrait.

In this, Lewis is careful not to deny the power of the personal. Instead, he situates it, contextualizes it, and corrects our misunderstanding of its limits. Sources of knowledge such as the Bible and the creeds are both "less real" and "less exciting" than experience, but they have the capacity to move beyond the elementary and myopic notions that sometimes mislead us. In other words, maps allow us to correct course. If religion by experience alone risks

[33]Lewis, *Mere Christianity*, 153-55.
[34]Lewis, *Mere Christianity*, 153.

yielding only a vague creed "all about feeling God in nature, and so on," then maps allow us to discover how it is that the joys of a scenic landscape might draw us into the riches of historic Christian faith.[35]

Revolutionary Poetics

Here we encounter a second—and even more powerful—stream of influence that shaped C. S. Lewis's understanding of the Christian faith: the British Romantic movement. On the Continent, Romanticism produced a wide-ranging literature that gave fresh, if disparate, emphasis to feeling, experience, and intuition in writings by authors such as Johann Wolfgang von Goethe, Novalis, and Heinrich Heine in Germany and Jean-Jacques Rousseau and François-René de Chateaubriand in France. This is the same European Romanticism within which Schleiermacher wrote his defense of Christianity and to which Hegel and his disciples eventually responded. Meanwhile, in Britain, Romanticism found its own adherents in writers who offered new perspectives on poetry and poetics in a time of political revolution and reform.

Lewis knew British Romantic literature very well indeed. His own relationship to the ideas of the British Romantics is complex and will be a subject for closer treatment in the next chapter, but for the moment we must trace at least the outlines of his engagement with this unique group of authors who shaped English literature between the late 1780s and the early 1830s. In fact, throughout his published and unpublished writings, references to Percy Bysshe Shelley, John Keats, William Blake, and many other Romantic-era authors abound. Some allusions to their works are

---

[35]Lewis, *Mere Christianity*, 155. A further discussion of the role of experience in Lewis might examine the notion of "numinous" religious experiences, described in Rudolf Otto's *The Idea of the Holy* (Eng. trans., 1923) and *Religious Essays*, which Lewis annotated and linked to Schleiermacher in a personal index (see C. S. Lewis Library collection, Wade); cf. David Werther and Susan Werther, eds., *C. S. Lewis's List: The Ten Books That Influenced Him Most* (New York: Bloomsbury, 2015).

obvious, while in other cases he throws a veil over his sources as if to obscure an influence.

Lewis's earliest acquaintance with the British Romantics came during his time as a student. As a professor, he recommended that students read and obtain as many of the great, "long" authors as possible: "as much reading and book-buying as you can possibly afford without getting tired or bankrupt," he told one correspondent.[36] His list of essential authors for the serious student includes many Romantic-era notables—Wordsworth, Coleridge, Byron, Keats, Shelley— and some who were favorites in his own library, such as Charles Lamb, William Hazlitt, Thomas De Quincey, and Jane Austen.[37] Not all were equal in his eyes, of course; at the close of Byron's *Don Juan*, Lewis memorably quipped, "Never again!"[38] Nevertheless, these were authors he read and reread (including Byron), and they crucially shaped Lewis's thinking about language, literature, and faith.

Two English Romantics stand out for special notice: William Wordsworth (1770–1850) and Samuel Taylor Coleridge (1772–1834). Best known for the poetic experiment that resulted in the publication of *Lyrical Ballads* (1798), their work remains a watershed contribution to the movement, arising from the *annus mirabilis*, the year of wonders, between 1797 and 1798, when their collaboration produced some of the best-loved poems ever written in the English language. During this remarkably productive period, these young men (alongside Wordsworth's sister Dorothy) rambled across the Quantock Hills of England's West Country and produced the work that first introduced English readers to an abandoned abbey, an albatross-laden mariner, and the strange sight of

---

[36] *CLCSL* 3.1571 (July 8, 1947).

[37] *CLCSL* 3.1571 (July 8, 1947).

[38] C. S. Lewis, *Surprised by Joy: The Shape of My Early Life* (Boston: Mariner, 2012), 214; cf. Lewis's personal library copy, which allows us to date his reading to February 1924: Lord Byron, *Don Juan*, ed. Ernest Hartley Coleridge (London: J. Murray, 1906), 612 (C. S. Lewis Library collection, Wade).

a wretched woman mourning by an old thorn bush. These were radical poets in tumultuous times—a season of revolution and change when war with France, the rise of Napoleon, terror, dissent, and political and religious strife reoriented the cultural landscape.

Not only in their poetry but also in their prose, Wordsworth and Coleridge signaled the new poetic sensibility with a depth of focus on feeling and imagination in the arts. When Wordsworth later wrote of their aims in the preface to the third edition of *Lyrical Ballads* (1800), he fostered the idea of a poet as "a man speaking to men: a man, it is true, endued with more lively sensibility, more enthusiasm and tenderness, who has a greater knowledge of human nature, and a more comprehensive soul, than are supposed to be common among mankind."[39] Such poetic activity depends on feeling, for poetry itself is "the spontaneous overflow of powerful feelings," and the poet's work is "to bring his feelings near to those of the persons whose feelings he describes."[40]

Figure 1.7. William Wordsworth

The poetic emphasis on feeling corresponds to a revitalized philosophy of the artistic imagination. In past centuries, imagination often suffered under a cloud of suspicion. The apostle Paul had warned against "every high thing that exalteth itself against the knowledge of God" (2 Cor 10:5), and many in the tradition feared

---

[39]William Wordsworth, "Preface to *Lyrical Ballads*," in *Wordsworth's Poetry and Prose*, Norton critical ed., ed. Nicholas Halmi (New York: Norton, 2014), 85.
[40]Wordsworth, "Preface," 92, 86.

the potential for self-deception in the unfettered delusion that imaginative activity could so easily generate.[41] By contrast, British Romantics picked up on German philosophical developments to adopt a more positive assessment of the imagination, likening the creative work of the artist to the creativity of God.

Coleridge famously defined the primary and secondary senses of imagination in his *Biographia Literaria* (1817), distinguishing between the creative perceptivity of the primary imagination—"a repetition in the finite mind of the eternal act of creation"—and the willed creativity of the secondary imagination: "It dissolves, diffuses, dissipates, in order to re-create; or where this process is rendered impossible, yet still at all events it struggles to idealize and to unify. It is essentially *vital*, even as all objects (*as* objects) are essentially fixed and dead."[42] Such a definition drew deep from the Neoplatonic wells of the Christian tradition, likening the vocation of the artist to the operations of the divine in the formation of all creation.

Lewis studied Wordsworth and Coleridge intensely during

Figure 1.8. Samuel Taylor Coleridge

his earliest years as a student, and they remained steadfast companions throughout his life. At first, he seems to have disliked Wordsworth's poetry, but by age twenty, he reported to Arthur

---

[41]For a review and defense of the theological imagination, see my "A Theology of Imagination," in Barbeau and McGowin, *God and Wonder*, 13-29.

[42]Samuel Taylor Coleridge, *Biographia Literaria*, ed. James Engell and W. Jackson Bate (Princeton, NJ: Princeton University Press, 1983), 1.304.

Greeves of a gradual change of heart. He had read Wordsworth's long autobiographical poem, *The Prelude*, and discovered with unexpected delight his enjoyment: "You will perhaps be surprised to hear that I am reading 'The Prelude' by way of graduating in Wordsworth-ism. What's even funnier, I rather like it!"[43]

The youthful Lewis comes off a bit smug in his earliest appraisal of Wordsworth, judging the poet with unflappable, youthful conviction. Over time, however, this attitude changed significantly. In fact, his "graduating in Wordsworth-ism" corresponded to a deeper longing to write poetry of his own. On the blank pages at the back of Lewis's personal copy of *The Shorter Poems of William Wordsworth* (1917), he even tried his hand at writing lines that meditate on death:

> Death has called to heel
> All sound: cut short the thunder in mid peel
> Laid dumbness upon every tongue: the shout
> Of millions like a puff'd flame is gone out
> Follows the darkness closing like a chest,
> No light, no sound, no thought, impartial rest
> For each frayed sense. Oh never any more
> Will cockcrow + reveille at their door
> Come stirring. No hard duty shall have power
> Forever to break on them for one hour[44]

These previously unknown and unpublished lines—thematically reminiscent of World War I poets such as Siegfried Sassoon and Wilfred Owen—personify Death as a master calling brute creation to obeisance. Death hems in the soldiers, encircling them within the darkness. Written in a somewhat uneven iambic pentameter

---

[43]*CLCSL* 1.466 (to Arthur Greeves, September 18, 1919).
[44]Marginalia by C. S. Lewis, in William Wordsworth, *The Shorter Poems of William Wordsworth: Poetry and Drama*, Everyman's Library (London: Dent & Sons, 1917), rear verso free endpaper and inside rear recto flyleaf (C. S. Lewis Library collection, Wade); for a full transcription of these previously unpublished poems, see the appendix.

(a staple in Wordsworth's poetics), the series of couplets explores grief and loss in simple, rhyming lines that reflect Lewis's own experience of war and the haphazard destruction of life.

Whatever the literary merit of these and other lines in his marginal scrawl at the back of his copy of Wordsworth, they are an indication that the Romantics inspired and motivated Lewis's early poetic efforts. Indeed, appreciative references to Wordsworth's works pervade Lewis's writing. In both published prose and personal correspondence, Wordsworth appears and reappears in Lewis's writings, culminating in the decision to title his own autobiography after Wordsworth's celebrated poem, "Surprised by Joy."[45]

We also know that Lewis studied Coleridge's poetry with similar care and could recall apt lines from memory throughout his life. As early as 1915, while still a teenager, Lewis mentions "Christabel" and "The Rime of the Ancient Mariner," recommending them to Arthur Greeves, and in subsequent years refers to "Kubla Khan," "Christabel," and other works regularly.[46] Lewis even documents how, during his first meeting with W. B. Yeats, a reference to Coleridge came to mind as he sheepishly prepared to join the vigorous conversation. Lewis was overawed on the occasion—he was still in his early twenties—and Yeats had terrified the "room into silence" as he pronounced on all matter of eighteenth-century literature.[47] Luckily Lewis held his tongue, for Yeats disclaimed the reference to Coleridge in the strongest terms almost at the same moment Lewis hoped to introduce it. Yet, forty years later, Lewis still quoted lines from "Christabel" to comfort his American correspondent (the so-called American Lady) Mary

---

[45]Though, notably, he claimed the title was incidental to its interpretation (*CLCSL* 3.614, June 1, 1955). On the relationship between these works, see chapter two.

[46]*CLCSL* 1.138 (July 24, 1915), 1.460 (July 14, 1919), 1.466 (September 18, 1919), 1.538 (April 20, 1921), 1 484 (April 11, 1920).

[47]*CLCSL* 1.532 (March 14, 1921).

Willis Shelburne, after learning of her most recent predicament: "to be wroth with one we love / Doth work like madness in the brain."[48]

The compositions of Wordsworth and Coleridge had a direct bearing on English religious life in the nineteenth century. In fact, some believed their poetry and prose had been inspired by overtly pietistic sources, leaving them open to charges of religious fanaticism (a topic I will take up in the next chapter). For now, I will only note that the emphasis on feeling and imagination in such poets brought fresh interest in the role of personal experience.

The Sublime Waterfall

Thus far, I have established two traditions of late eighteenth- and early nineteenth-century Romanticism with which C. S. Lewis was intimately familiar. On the one hand, the German philosophical and theological tradition after Immanuel Kant had wrestled with the relationship between subjectivity and objectivity, leaving the existence of God in a state of limbo. On the other, a similar pietistic impulse led British Romantics such as Wordsworth and Coleridge to connect the work of the poet to feeling and the creative imagination. Little more than a century after these pivotal writings, no adequate defense of Christianity could fail to grapple with the relationship between personal experience and claims of a universally accessible, "objective" truth. The foregoing account is essential for understanding one of C. S. Lewis's most well-known and misunderstood prose works: *The Abolition of Man*.

In 1939, Lewis read a new publication by two Australian educators. The green cloth cover, perhaps symbolizing the youthful disposition of its prospective readers, enveloped a carefully constructed argument about reading and writing for students. The

---

[48]"Christabel," lines 412-13, in Samuel Taylor Coleridge, *Poetical Works*, ed. J. C. C. Mays (Princeton, NJ: Princeton University Press, 2001), 1.1.496; cf. *CLCSL* 3.1203 (October 28, 1960).

so-called *Green Book*, as it is now widely known, was originally published by Alec King and Martin Ketley under the title *The Control of Language: A Critical Approach to Reading and Writing*.[49]

I have held Lewis's personal copy of *The Green Book* in my own hands. While many volumes in Lewis's library contain only scant markings—slight editorial notes, cross-references, or occasional summary observations—this slim volume includes numerous annotations, signs of his frustration and disapproval with the authors. The now infamous title is almost universally understood as the key to Lewis's prophetic denunciation of an educational system that had replaced objective moral values with feelings alone—precisely the opposite of Professor Inch's argument about Lewis's worrying subjectivity!

Some have thought that Lewis's argument in *The Abolition of Man* is altogether bewildering. For while Lewis begins the book with a rather confounding discussion of false ideas about language, readers gradually recognize that Lewis wishes to evaluate the relationship between universal moral values and personal experience. The close of his first chapter begins to signal this larger, ethical concern: "We make men without chests" but "are shocked to find traitors in our midst."[50] These are fighting words for Lewis, to be sure. Yet, in case any readers have missed his point, he opens the second chapter with the strongest possible condemnation, claiming that students formed by *The Green Book* will inevitably destroy the society in which they are raised.[51]

In *The Abolition of Man*, Lewis contends against such a fate by advocating for the existence of objective truth. Lewis claims that all

---

[49] Alec King and Martin Ketley, *The Control of Language: A Critical Approach to Reading and Writing* (London: Longmans, Green, 1939) (cf. Lewis's personal copy in the C. S. Lewis Library collection, Wade).

[50] C. S. Lewis, *The Abolition of Man, or Reflections on Education with Special Reference to the Teaching of English in the Upper Forms of Schools* (New York: HarperCollins, 2000), 26.

[51] Lewis, *Abolition of Man*, 27.

have access to a knowledge of universal values through what he calls the "Tao." This "Way," as he names it, depends not on our feelings or instincts for its existence or justification. Rather, the Tao names the universals that some traditions identify with the natural law.[52] The law is an innate idea and not based on deduction or argumentation. Thus, he refers in the appendix to laws ranging from beneficence, justice, and mercy to duties toward family and the wider community. For Lewis, then, the law depends not on the whimsy of individuals or the variances between communities but that which serves as the basis of all value systems that exist in any time, place, or religion.[53]

Nevertheless, for all its strengths as an argument for the existence of a universal moral law, *The Abolition of Man* opens with a surprisingly confusing treatment of language, centering on a discussion of *The Green Book* and an obscure illustration from the life of Romantic poet Samuel Taylor Coleridge. Lewis claims that the authors of *The Green Book* (whom he identifies as "Gaius" and "Titius") repeat the story of an encounter at a waterfall, where Coleridge met two tourists and engaged in a brief conversation. One of the tourists, overawed by the waterfall, called it "sublime," while the other dubbed it "pretty." Lewis explains that the authors of *The Green Book* wrongly suggest that the reason Coleridge prefers "sublime" to "pretty" comes down to Coleridge's feelings about the waterfall. Here's the relevant passage in *The Control of Language*:

> Why did Coleridge think the one word was exactly right, and the other exactly wrong? Obviously not because the one adjective described correctly, as we say, a quality of the water or the rocks or the landscape, and the other adjective described

---

[52]Lewis, *Abolition of Man*, 43.

[53]Notably, Lewis claims that not only the Greeks and Romans knew such things but also those in ancient Babylon and across the populations of twentieth-century Asia. Lewis was no expert in world religions, but his library provides direct evidence of his studies in the Qur'an, the Gita, and other religious philosophies.

this quality incorrectly. It is not as if the man had said "That is brown" (referring, say, to the water) and the woman (also referring to the water) had added, "Yes, it is green." No, Coleridge thought "sublime" exactly the right word, because it was associated in his mind with the emotion he was himself feeling as he looked at the waterfall in its setting of rock and landscape; and he thought "pretty" exactly the wrong word, because it was associated with feelings quite different from those he was actually feeling at the time, and with feelings that, to his way of thinking, no sensitive person would ever have while looking at such a sight.[54]

King and Ketley argue that words such as *brown* and *blue* differ from *sublime* and *pretty* because the former communicate features of the thing itself (the waterfall), whereas the latter express only the feelings or emotions of the viewer (whether Coleridge's or the tourists').

Lewis's marginalia in *The Control of Language* indicate that such claims leave pupils unable to name emotions, for the interior state of being is lost in favor of external realities alone. In fact, Lewis worries that such a position reduces any writing about emotion to mere propaganda. When the authors claim, "The difficulty of thinking and writing about idealism and ideals is that these words do not stand for anything definite, as the word 'sofa' stands for something definite," Lewis counters: "They do when I use 'em!"[55]

The opening of *The Abolition of Man* signals the deep Romanticism of Lewis. On a most basic level, the illustration is one that shows familiarity with Romantic literature—though I should note that Lewis need not have read the illustration in Coleridge to pick up on the example, for he had read and noted it in *The Control of Language*, and the authors themselves most likely derived it from

---

[54]King and Ketley, *Control of Language*, 17-18.
[55]Lewis marginalia in King and Ketley, *Control of Language*, 92 (C. S. Lewis Library collection, Wade).

Dorothy Wordsworth's *Recollections of a Tour in Scotland, A.D. 1803* (published in 1874). I am also not referring to the simple fact that the first chapter of *The Abolition of Man* contains a surprising number of references to British Romantic literature—though if the thrust of his argument was to make a case *against* Romanticism, it surely is surprising that Lewis's chapter repeatedly cites the works of not only Coleridge but also such beloved Romantics as William Wordsworth, Charles Lamb, and Percy Bysshe Shelley.

Rather, a Romantic argument runs throughout *The Abolition of Man* in Lewis's insistence that our personal experiences not only matter but also correspond in a meaningful way to the world around us. While many students will find themselves roused emotionally by cultural propaganda, many more need to be roused from cold (and seemingly rational) listlessness.[56] Such a reality requires something of educators that Lewis feared had been lost, namely, a pedagogy of personal development. Objective reality and subjective experience may not always be congruous, but education involves formation. Students must learn to identify when their feelings are incongruous with the thing itself: "The little human animal will not at first have the right responses. It must be trained to feel pleasure, liking, disgust, and hatred at those things which really are pleasant, likeable, disgusting, and hateful."[57]

Moreover, Lewis's discussion of the sublime waterfall—surely an obscure reference to most of his audience—was no accident. Readers familiar with the Romantic tradition will immediately recognize that Lewis's use of the term *sublime* recalls one of the foremost controversies of British Romantic literature, namely, the relationship between the external, objective world and the internal, subjective feelings. For the Romantics, influenced by the writings of Edmund Burke, Immanuel Kant, and others, the word *sublime*

---

[56]Lewis, *Abolition of Man*, 13.
[57]Lewis, *Abolition of Man*, 16, cf. 21.

resounds with meaning—philosophically, aesthetically, and theologically—since these authors sought to understand the relationship between the objective and subjective.

In addition to serving as a reminder of Lewis's own indebtedness to British Romantic aesthetics, the sublime waterfall also intimates a peculiarly religious concern. For some, a sublime waterfall is one that overwhelms the viewer with its majesty or threatens personal well-being, but such a feature of the landscape might also lead to wonderment when faced with the transcendent mystery of God's creative power. The sublime identifies our inability to name the numinous—a mystery beyond the capacity of language. Just such a power is revealed in the encounter with nature that Wordsworth describes in *The Prelude* (1805), after the poet ascended Mount Snowdon:

> A meditation rose in me that night
> Upon the lonely Mountain when the scene
> Had passed away, and it appeared to me
> The perfect image of a mighty Mind,
> Of one that feeds upon infinity,
> That is exalted by an under-presence,
> The sense of God, or whatsoe'er is dim
> Or vast in its own being . . .[58]

It's not hard to see why the language of the sublime crossed easily into the language of the numinous—the mysterious language of encounter with a holy God.

In taking up the sublime at the commencement of *The Abolition of Man*, Lewis thereby engages in a distinctly Romantic debate. Neither Lewis nor the Romantics before him sought to erase either universal values or personal experience. Instead, Lewis feared that

---

[58]William Wordsworth, *The Prelude* (1805), book 13.66-73, in *Wordsworth's Poetry and Prose*, 367. On Coleridge and the sublime, by comparison, see Murray J. Evans, *Coleridge's Sublime Later Prose and Recent Theory: Kristeva, Adorno, Rancière* (Cham, Switzerland: Palgrave Macmillan, 2023).

the authors of *The Green Book* risked obliterating the interior life as ephemeral when the true goal of education was to help others recognize the congruity or incongruity of the heart.

The Limits of Experience

When members of Wheaton College engaged in debate over C. S. Lewis, they were asking questions about the legacy of the Romantic movement itself. Appeals to the role of imagination in the pursuit of truth risked imperiling the Christian faith to the whimsy of individualism and subjectivity. When Morris Inch contested Clyde Kilby, asserting that Lewis dallied in a Romanticism with "Shades of Schleiermacher," he appeared to have fundamentally misunderstood Lewis's commitment to universal values. I think Inch picked up on something that is easily overlooked in Lewis's writings, for he not only embraced the power of imagination but also recognized the vitality of the interior life as a key aspect of all human knowing.

In both *Mere Christianity* and *The Abolition of Man*, Lewis engages in arguments that reflect the modern temperament and disputes over the ability of the individual to perceive and understand truth. Lewis does not ignore religious feeling—he builds on it and seeks a means to correct it. Yet references to the subjective inform many of Lewis's other works, too. For instance, in *The Screwtape Letters*, the theme appears repeatedly in letters devoted to rationality, prayer, and the temptations surrounding individual experience. Whereas in *The Problem of Pain*, Lewis directly counters the traditions of left-wing Hegelianism in his efforts to undermine self-idolatry, wish-fulfillment, and a broader cultural tendency toward materialism.

Indeed, such a tendency to consider the relationship between what some Romantics called the "objective" and "subjective" reflects the most profound and pressing questions of his own life—a time when world wars and the destruction of innocents weighed heavily on the minds of both Lewis and his contemporaries. Without the ability to appeal to personal experience, he risked speaking about faith in the language of cold rationalism. Yet without universal moral values, Lewis thought there would be no way to condemn the Germans, the Japanese, or any other power that might assert itself by military strength. In such a world, judging something good or right would amount to little more than a socially constructed feeling.[59]

Indeed, these remain questions that face people in our day. Can I trust my own experience? How do my experiences of faith relate to those of other people? Who (or what) has the authority to challenge, correct, or augment my religious beliefs? Such perennial questions mean that any author who takes up "feeling" or "experience" or "the numinous" as a religious category—as a means of verifying belief—runs the risk of severe criticism.

Writing in a decidedly less optimistic age than his forebears, Lewis recognized the limits of arguments from experience. If apologists for experience in the nineteenth century saw new possibilities in the advancing kingdom of God, defenders of faith in the twentieth recognized the existential threat of human self-interest. Sin, seemingly forgotten in the optimism of a prior generation, now appeared as the most compelling obstacle to any unfettered experience of the divine or any wholly rational access to truth. As I will explain later, Lewis recognized this limitation and attempted to account for it.[60]

Lewis's preoccupation with subjectivity is the legacy of Romanticism. That his argument turns from personal experience to the universality of an objective law is not a denial of Romanticism but

[59]C. S. Lewis, "The Poison of Subjectivism," in *The Seeing Eye, and Other Selected Essays from "Christian Reflections,"* ed. Walter Hooper (New York: Ballentine Books, 1967), 101, 99-112; cf. Jean Bethke-Elshtain, "The Abolition of Man: C. S. Lewis's Prescience Concerning Things to Come," in *C. S. Lewis as Philosopher: Truth, Goodness, and Beauty*, 2nd ed., ed. David J. Baggett, Gary R. Habermas, and Jerry L. Walls (Lynchburg, VA: Liberty University Press, 2017), 77-87.

[60]Gilbert Meilaender, "On Moral Knowledge," in *The Cambridge Companion to C. S. Lewis*, ed. Robert MacSwain and Michael Ward (Cambridge: Cambridge University Press, 2010), 119-31.

an extension of it. For example, many know that Coleridge appealed to the subjective in his defense of the Bible, stating that "whatever *finds* me" bears witness to its inspiration, but fewer realize that Coleridge saw the experience of such inspiration as a mirror of what might be called the "objective" truth of the Scriptures.[61] Similarly, Lewis's discussion of the moral law might be confused as a rejection of the interior life (the "whatever *finds* me" part of faith), but I think this is a matter of emphasis. Lewis often begins with the individual to point his readers toward the general, building on the foundation of the personal to recognize that which is beyond the personal.

Lewis's place in the history of modern thought should be reassessed. As I have argued throughout this first chapter, C. S. Lewis was not the hostile opponent of Romanticism that he might at first glance appear. Rather, Lewis ought to be regarded as the last in a prestigious heritage. Chronologically, his life began long after the end of the Romantic movement in Britain, but Lewis's prose writings cannot be understood without reference to their debates and interests. The Romantics were his abiding dialogue partners, and reading him as an inheritor of their legacy reshapes our understanding of his thought.

In fact, as I will show in the next two chapters, the Romantic element is one of the most compelling aspects of Lewis's contribution to modern thought and, I think, a considerable part of his ongoing appeal to readers today. Yet Lewis's fear about popular conceptions of Romanticism led him to prevaricate and redirect readers, always deflecting attention away from the movement when we might otherwise expect him to embrace it. In the next chapter, such discomfort appears again and again in his effort to write about his own life. Surprisingly, a rather startling anxiety surfaces as Lewis writes personally about faith and memory, leading him to make one of the most paradoxical claims in the history of modern autobiography.

---

[61]Samuel Taylor Coleridge, *Confessions of an Inquiring Spirit*, Fortress Texts in Modern Theology (Philadelphia: Fortress, 1988), 26.

RESPONSE
Sarah Borden

It has been a joy both to read carefully—and then listen to—Jeffrey Barbeau's work on C. S. Lewis's relationship to Romanticism. His opening history tracing Wheaton College faculty responses to C. S. Lewis was illuminating (and oddly encouraging), and his account of Lewis's engagement with German philosophy has helped open up new ways for reading Lewis; I am delighted to have learned through Dr. Barbeau's evidence that Lewis was far more thorough in his study of the philosophers of the last centuries than at least I had been aware! Of particular interest to me, however, is the question animating Dr. Barbeau's paper on Lewis and the "Romantic heresy": What role do emotions play in the pursuit of truth? This is a question of profound significance and deeply relevant to both our personal and theoretical lives.

The question of the "truth of feelings" is an old one, showing up, for example, in vivid form in Augustine's *Confessions* as he explores emotional contagion, discernment of emotional states, and the relation of feeling and knowing. Ultimately, Augustine claims that, although knowing and feeling differ, we cannot *know* rightly if we do not *love* rightly. This relationship between knowing and feeling is core to the ancient Augustinian vision—and it is a vision that has been lost in much of our contemporary world.

There is a long story that could be told about how knowledge and truth got separated from our feelings and emotions, and Dr. Barbeau points to several pieces of this story with the European Enlightenment and the German Romantic response. But, even more importantly, Jeffrey Barbeau paints a portrait of Lewis as an Augustinian on this point and perhaps even a significant figure in retrieving that ancient Christian vision. Dr. Barbeau argues that C. S. Lewis neither embraces emotions as simply a way to capture attention or give color to his claims (as J. Randall Springer argues in his "defense" of Lewis), nor appeals to emotions in a way that will ultimately compromise one's pursuit of what is true (as Morris Inch fears). Rather, Lewis is, on the issue of emotions, truly working with and helping retrieve the older Augustinian vision that our knowing and our loving work in tandem.

This project is both deeply exciting and timely, and I would like to offer a small contribution to Dr. Barbeau's way of reading Lewis. Dr. Barbeau tells the story of Lewis's engagement with emotions and truth by placing Lewis within conversations: first, on the European continent, including Hegelian notions of the progress of reason, Feuerbachian reductions of religious feelings to human psychology, and a Schleiermacherian retrieval of the Romantic tradition for theological conversations; then, second, with the British Romantics, including particularly Wordsworth and Coleridge. I suspect Dr. Barbeau is exactly right to focus on each of these two intersecting lines. In these brief comments, however, I would like to pause for just a bit longer with the European philosophical conversations.

There are at least three developments in the German conversations on knowledge and emotions, especially as developed by the twentieth-century German phenomenologists, that fit particularly well with themes in Lewis's way of working out his "Augustinian answer." These are, first, concerns that the very language of subjectivity and objectivity that has become dominant in modernity have contributed to a crisis in our ability to think well about truth; second, that there are paths forward for articulating better models, including greater focus on emotions themselves and attention to intersubjectivity. Both of these paths are ones taken by Lewis, and putting him into greater conversation with those emphases in phenomenology may prove productive. Finally, I would like to raise a brief caution, one that both Augustine and Lewis were well aware of and that should be part of any substantive engagement with questions of truth and emotions.

A WORD

First, a word on terms to use: Dr. Barbeau draws from language common throughout modernity, distinguishing the "subjective" from the "objective." He quotes Morris Inch's concerns that Lewis, in embracing the subjective, may lose objective fact, and he describes how Lewis's attention to our subjective experiences can "correspond in a meaningful way to the objective world around us." Although Dr. Barbeau need not be guilty of a problematic version of this language, Enlightenment-era thinkers had long used the term *subjective* to refer to what is individual, personal, and unreliable, in contrast to the *objective*, which is taken to be true, impersonal, and reliable.[1] Given this legacy, language of the subjective and objective is already part of a heritage that has questions about what positive role personal feelings could possibly play in objectivity.

Although language of the subjective and objective may have a role, the twentieth-century phenomenologists such as Edmund Husserl and Martin Heidegger pointed out in particularly clear ways that one cannot sharply separate the two; there is no access to what is "objective" except through personal, subjective experience. This is as true for claims about math and tables as it is for claims about a waterfall's

---

[1] One might look at René Descartes's explicit rejection of tradition and other "subjective" prejudices or Francis Bacon's analysis of various "idols" of the mind. Once subjectivity and objectivity were sharply distinguished by the early modern and Enlightenment eras, the philosophical question became how one gets from subjectivity to objectivity. Many Enlightenment thinkers celebrated the universal power of Reason as the only reliable bridge, while others focused on distinctively universal feelings, empirical or sense experience, etc. Each answer, however, carried suspicion regarding the very type of emotions and feelings Lewis discusses, considering them as unlikely bridges. One concern I have, however, is whether we should have ever accepted the sharp separation of subjectivity and objectivity in the first place, rather than thinking in terms of *truth* or other terms less liable to spatialized visions of the person and knowledge.

beauty. There is nothing that can be said or judged to be true about a table that has not been experienced or personally accessed by someone. Any attempt to sharply separate the "objective" from all subjectivity is impossible, and many of the early modern attempts to radically limit objectivity to simply what is accessible via some refined sense of reason or via one's five senses suffer from incoherence or arbitrariness.[2] The question should not be "How do we get the subjective *out* of our objective claims?"[3] but, rather, "How and on the basis of *which aspects of* each of our subjective, personal experiences can one make responsible, evidenced truth claims?"

Addressing this latter question well will require many steps and likely a thoroughly developed theory of knowledge, but at minimum, one might distinguish notions of subjectivity from a subcategory of the "merely subjective." Not all that is subjective is merely subjective. The subjective or first-personal includes anything a subject might experience, which—for most people—includes experiences such as seeing, hearing, and tasting as well as feeling. People see tables, hear the wind in the trees, taste sweet desserts, and feel joy at good news. Our visual, aural, and taste experiences can reveal true things, such as the features of a table, the wind, and this slice of chocolate cake. They can also, however, be merely subjective, such as when I see the something before me spinning while I whip around in the wind or suffer from dizziness, or when the cake tastes flat rather than sweet as one suffers the side effects

---

[2]Defending this claim lies well beyond the limits of a brief response, but the pall David Hume's skepticism placed on early modern epistemology makes clear the depth of the challenge, a skepticism Kant may have avoided in name but not in relation to projects such as classic metaphysics.

[3]Morris Inch's worries about contaminating "objective fact" with "subjective feeling" articulate well the problematic version of the question. I take Inch's fact/feeling dichotomy to be particularly problematic, insofar as fact is identified with truth while feeling with individual, personal, and/or passing experience. But equally problematic is the identification of objectivity with facts and subjectivity with feelings, as if subjectivity had nothing to do with facts and objectivity nothing to do with feelings.

of COVID-19. In the latter such cases, my personal experiences have become *merely* subjective.

Our emotions or experiences of feelings, like experiences of seeing and tasting, are first-personal and subjective, but they are not thereby merely subjective. To argue that being personal or subjective per se is sufficient for being unreliable or non-truth-functional will cut against far more than the truth-orientation of feelings. The key question should not be whether feelings are personal or subjective but whether they are merely subjective. And defenders of the truth-orientation of feelings, like Dr. Barbeau and Lewis himself, can make use of the similarities of feelings with all other first-personal experience to argue that the subjectivity of emotions may well be relevant to grasping certain objective features of reality.

Two Paths

This leads, second, to the question of *how* one should attend to emotions in one's pursuit of truth—of what path one should take to move through subjectivity to what is true. The early twentieth-century phenomenologists, particularly Edmund Husserl and his students, were deeply interested in the nature of subjectivity and its relation to our grasp of objectivity or truth, so interested in fact that Husserl saw the post-Hegelian European conversations on the topic to be in a state of crisis. For Husserl, key to moving forward is detailed attention to our first-personal experiences, and this attention to a first-personal analysis of our feelings animated the work of Edith Stein, Max Scheler, Dietrich von Hildebrand, and Martin Heidegger.

Such a turn *to* the personal and emotional appears similarly in Lewis's work. In the opening chapters of *Mere Christianity*, as Lewis discusses the Moral Law or law of decent behavior, he says that we *feel* that law pressing on us.[4] His description is not of someone

---

[4]See, for example, C. S. Lewis, *Mere Christianity* (New York: Macmillan, 1977), 21.

intellectually grasping the moral law and then, because of that knowledge, coming also to feel it. Rather, he argues that even those who might intellectually deny the Moral Law still *feel* that law, so much so that the individuals *feel* a need to make excuses for their failure to follow it.

As Lewis develops his argument in the opening sections, he addresses a series of objections, including the objection that the Moral Law could simply be reduced to a "herd instinct." In order to respond to this objection, Lewis distinguishes a number of differing types of feelings, articulating how we experience instinctual drives versus how we experience, or feel, the Moral Law. That is, he does not point to something *other* than our feelings but calls us to look more closely *at* our feelings. Making clear distinctions among differing types of feelings and describing (and naming) how they are experienced is core to Lewis's response. Lewis does not give a detailed map of our emotions in *Mere Christianity,* but attention to our emotions—or the discernment of emotional states—is nonetheless at the heart of Lewis's arguments there.

Things can, of course, go wrong in the analysis of our feelings. One might, for example, not have a very good set of names for one's differing feelings or modes of experiencing. One might also fail to notice all that one is experiencing affectively.[5] Or one might live in a community or family that does not encourage or in any way celebrate attentiveness to emotions. It is not easy to read well one's own feelings. (Nor, incidentally, is it easy to read well one's taste, smell, or other sense experiences, as expert sommeliers and perfumers make clear.)

Lewis's advice appears to be, first, to slow down. Name and notice what we are in fact experiencing. Doing so is essential for learning

---

[5]And we certainly should also ask whether all affective experiences or feelings are emotions. For the sake of this brief essay, I am using *emotions* and *feelings* interchangeably, but I am not committed to this identity ultimately. At the very least, I would want to distinguish, within affective experiences, *moods* and *emotions*.

to distinguish what might be merely subjective (or perhaps a type of preference) in contrast to what reveals something quite different. Lewis's response to the objection that the Moral Law is simply a herd instinct turns on the ability to discern differences in feelings and affective experiences, and he calls us to note the features by which certain feelings reveal objectivity and a Moral Law.

This move in Lewis shares much with Augustine's project in book III of the *Confessions*. Careful discernment and self-knowledge are necessary. If we do not know what we are feeling, if we cannot distinguish those emotions from other, related feelings, we are liable to misread them. This inattentiveness would make it easy to confuse a moral feeling with something that is merely subjective (such as, perhaps, a passing mood or a mere individually conditioned preference), or it could lead us to conflate in problematic ways differing parts of an experience. Lewis's claim appears to be—like Augustine's—that, via attention and adequate language and categories, one can discern rightly *what* one is feeling and whether it is merely subjective or truth-conducive. This project of carefully discerning our various emotional states and then arguing that certain objective truths are grasped through certain types of emotional experiences is, I think, an essential (and fascinating) argument. It is also central to fully defending the thesis on Lewis's account of emotions that Dr. Barbeau's analysis points us to.

A second feature of Lewis's path through the question of emotions and truth likewise echoes another theme emphasized by the twentieth-century students of Edmund Husserl, particularly Edith Stein: in order to discern well what is merely subjective versus truth conducive, one must also attend to the role of intersubjective experiences. In answering the objection of the "hard-bitten officer" in *Mere Christianity,* Lewis moves from one's personal experiences to a type of coalescing of the many perspectives of others, which enables the drawing of a map. Such an "interpersonally" developed or intersubjectively informed vision provides a key feature for articulating what can be truth-conducive in one's personal experiences and what may not be.

Accounts of intersubjective experience were not a mainstay of Descartes or the early moderns, and the idealism dominating Hegel and his German successors often gave little room for the nuanced distinctions necessary to giving a fully adequate account of how we can experience others' personal experiences and can thus incorporate them into a full epistemology. But I think Lewis is correct that attention to intersubjectivity will be crucial, and I would commend the nuanced and detailed analyses that have developed particularly in the last century among the European phenomenologists, including especially Husserl, Stein, and the more recent commentators on these two.

A Caution

Finally, I would like to end with a caution. Dr. Barbeau cites Professor Morris Inch's concerns about the dangers of emotions and imagination. Augustine begins his own analysis in book III of the *Confessions* with "the sizzling and frying of unholy loves"[6]—and, as the prophet Jeremiah reminds us, "The heart is deceitful above all things" (Jer 17:9). For all the promise of moving through subjectivity to objectivity—and I do think this is both a promising and right move—Professor Morris Inch was not wrong to caution us about our emotions and the complications involved in reading and discerning well our states of heart.

Despite all the similarities, moving through subjectivity to objectivity (or from personal experiences to truth claims) surely must work at least somewhat differently for seeing versus feeling. If we treat our emotional lives as analogous to our perceptual

---

[6]*The Confessions of St. Augustine*, trans. Rex Warner (New York: Penguin Books, 1963), III.1.

lives—which is, I think, what Augustine and Lewis are doing—there is, nonetheless, something different in the discernment of emotional versus perceptional experiences. Our emotions are both more personal than seeing or hearing and also distinctively liable to go wrong in numerous ways. Thus, unpacking and evaluating the effects of sin on what one might call "the cognitive contributions of feelings" is central to Dr. Barbeau's project. I am optimistic that there is a way forward and one that does not require that one deem all emotions merely subjective. But the path from emotional "data" to objectivity has additional complications, and acknowledgment of those complications is crucial. Pursuing study of the objectivity and truth-orientation of emotions is not a job for the faint-hearted.

I am convinced by Dr. Barbeau both (1) that this is something significant about how Lewis treats emotions that has not yet been adequately unpacked and (2) that Lewis's use of the Romantics is central to his vision of emotions. But following Lewis in this project of showing how our emotions reveal truth—and how loving rightly is essential to knowing rightly—is no small task. It will fly in the face of assumptions shaping much of modernity, and it will take time, deep self-awareness, and adequate language and conceptual models, as well as, likely, substantive communal support and engagement. Recruiting the beauty of the Romantic poets seems wise, both for their insight and inspiration. Engaging as well the work of twentieth-century phenomenologists, especially the early phenomenologists focused on these very questions, may also prove productive. It is a path well worth traveling, even as it is one that has yet many miles to go.

Two

C. S. LEWIS AND THE
ANXIETY OF MEMORY

BURNED-OVER DISTRICT

Winter 1843. Writing in a neat, cursive script, a young woman begins to record what will eventually serve as one of the few lasting memorials of her life. There is little to distinguish this now-tattered daybook. The blue cloth cover measures twelve inches in height and nearly eight inches in width. Its brown spine has faded with time. Edges are worn, pages foxed with tan stains, and a few signs of dampness remind me that this monument will not last forever. *The Journal of Sarah Eliza Congdon* remains in many ways a mystery, but its contents detail the struggles of a young woman caught up in the revival fires that swept western New York in the mid-nineteenth century.

Opening the notebook, I quickly discover that it begins in the most ordinary way. Five years earlier, Sarah Congdon began to inscribe arithmetic lessons in these pages. There are samples of addition, subtraction, and long division. Word problems involving supplies to be purchased and debts to be paid. Interleaved within, I find a fragment of silk, perhaps the remainder of a dress she wore, with a delicate band of white along a single, unfrayed edge. More startling—and more delightful—is a lock of what I surmise is her own hair: a thin collection of straight, chestnut-brown strands that have been pressed into the crease between two pages.

From time to time, she wrote her name on a page: "Sarah Eliza Congdon's Book. Elmira NY. January 14. 1840. Chemung."[1] Elsewhere, the delicate script takes on a more serious, declarative character. In one case, bold, elegant letters stand out:

<blockquote>
Sarah Eliza Congdon.

Is my name.

America, is my nation;

Rhinebeck, is my native place.

And Christ is my salvation.[2]
</blockquote>

These signature lines are inscribed as a sacred act, a vindication of the self on earth and, hopefully, in heaven.

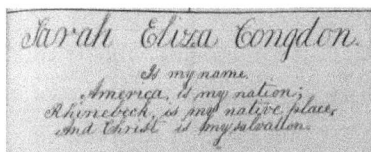

Figure 2.1. *The Journal of Sarah Eliza Congdon*

When Sarah Eliza Congdon began her *Journal* on February 1, 1843, however, the sure lines of a pupil gradually gave way to a less certain hand and voice. She opens neither with confident assertions of self-regard nor religious conviction but instead with existential questions: "Where am I? What am I doing? Five years ago my Heavenly Father for the sake of his son, forgave me my sins. I thought that was sufficient, & stood still, and spiritually died."[3]

---

[1] *The Journal of Sarah Eliza Congdon*, unpublished notebook (ca. 1838–1845), Wheaton College Archives, p. 106. My profound thanks to Sarah Stanley, formerly an assistant professor and archivist in the Wheaton College Special Collections, for first alerting me to the journal.

[2] Congdon, *Journal*, 61.

[3] Congdon, *Journal*, 165.

The interrogative commencement of Sarah Congdon's *Journal* epitomizes the uncertainty of her soul as she grapples with experiences of faith. In these pages, she composes her identity, introducing readers to her own anxious voice and the doubt she harbors. Having once received forgiveness, Sarah Congdon now questions her standing before the heavenly throne:

> I have since had good desires, & have frequently determined by God's grace to lead a new life. At times, I thought I enjoyed a sense of the favor of the Lord. I can look back to one class meeting, where I was so lost in praise, that I closed my eyes, bowed my head, & thought my happy soul would thus stay, & sing herself away to everlasting bliss. I remember too once when I thought I was going to die, it created a sensation of great joy, but when I recovered from my faintness I cried at the disappointment. This could not have been far from a year from my conversion. When my heart was young and tender at the age of thirteen, I for a short time loved my Savior, & tried to do right, but my natural levity and rudeness, and my impetuous temper soon led me astray; I first admitted the tempter, as a tempter, then as a friend, but alas! I find him in my breast a rankling foe.[4]

Congdon continually upends a reader's anticipations in oscillating movements of confidence and uncertainty: the prospect of death holds hope but is dashed in the recovery that follows. Divine favor and inner peace meet with disappointment and discontent.

Years earlier, around the same time she first wrote her arithmetic lessons in this same book, Congdon thought herself good. She loved her Savior and attempted to live a moral life, but flippant levity and impoliteness got the better of her. By her own account, she was something of a hothead, prone to sudden bursts of anger.

---

[4]Congdon, *Journal*, 165.

And this restlessness, over and over again, points back to the loss of her mother and the ever-present prospect of death:

> For two years past, I have prayed sometimes once a day, because I feared to lay my head upon my pillow to sleep, without, & sometimes it has been entirely neglected. When I think of God, I fear his judgements, when I think of Christ, I am not ready to meet him in the air;—when I think of the Holy Spirit, I know I have insulted him, stifled my convictions & striven to escape his warnings. Oh! where am I? My mother in yon bright world sees not my wretched condition, or it would sully even her pure joys. Oh! shall it be that mother will ever forget she had a daughter Sarah? If I am lost, oh may she forget I ever lived.[5]

But Sarah Eliza Congdon is not forgotten. She lives on today through the journal she composed. In writing her life, this young woman participated in a long tradition of spiritual autobiography, preserving her memory in the leaves of an ordinary notebook.

Of her life and times, this much is clear: Sarah Eliza Congdon was born in the Hudson Valley town of Rhinebeck, New York, in June 1824. She remained there until she was perhaps eleven or twelve, when her family moved to Elmira in western New York. Her mother, the subject of several entries in Sarah's journal, died in 1830, leaving behind a husband, Hannibal, and several children, including at least two younger siblings and, later, other half-siblings from her father's second marriage.[6]

---

[5]Congdon, *Journal*, 165.
[6]Sylvester Congdon (1826–1868) experienced conversion (1843) and was subsequently admitted to ministry in the Methodist Episcopal Church (1847). Upon his death, Sylvester was remembered in the conference minutes as a man "endowed with a clear and comprehensive mind, marked conscientiousness, an ardent, genial temperament, and a deep spiritual nature." Mary Satchwell (Congdon) Hebard (1828–1915) was an abolitionist and co-laborer with Susan B. Anthony in the suffrage movement; Mary was among the group of women charged for illegally voting after registering in Rochester, NY.

More significantly, *The Journal of Sarah Eliza Congdon* reveals her spiritual journey. In May 1843, Congdon begins teaching in Southport, not far from Elmira, and visits a Presbyterian church. Finding that meeting "rather cool," Sarah turns to the local Methodist Episcopal Church, where she discovers a "warm-hearted and whole-souled" congregation.[7] In subsequent months, Congdon describes a fervent search for deeper faith: there are protracted meetings and camp meetings, quarterly meetings and watchnight services, love feasts and the sacrament. She depicts not only her own experiences but also those of fellow seekers around her: some are moved to tears, others to laughter or ecstatic joy, and a few are so touched by God's presence they can stand no more and appear "slain in the Lord."[8]

Figure 2.2. Jacques Gérard Milbert, *Camp Meeting of the Methodists in North America* (ca. 1819)

All the while, Sarah Eliza Congdon undulates in periods of confidence and self-loathing alike. She struggles with deep unhappiness

[7]Congdon, *Journal*, 169.
[8]Congdon, *Journal*, 169.

but finds in Christ a sure foundation: "Oh, how much Christ is worth to me! I am a poor, feeble, fallible mortal, & God is an ocean of purity; a heaven of love."[9] And though she endures many temptations, Sarah finally discovers the confident salvation and perfect love she had heard reported among so many others, proclaiming, "Glory to the Lord my Maker. Oh, how faithful! how true! My Redeemer is *my own, my own, my own*."[10]

What has the tattered diary of a young Methodist woman from the burned-over district of New York to do with an Oxbridge professor writing for publication a century later? In this chapter, I suggest C. S. Lewis draws on many of the same traditions of life writing in the composition of some of his most famous autobiographical works that inspired Sarah Congdon, with one key difference: the British Romantic literary tradition shaped C. S. Lewis's conception of spiritual autobiography.

In the first chapter, I traced Lewis's indebtedness to nineteenth-century theology and philosophy—from Schleiermacher to Feuerbach—and the emphasis on feeling and subjectivity that characterized the poetics of English Romantics such as William Wordsworth and Samuel Taylor Coleridge. Lewis knew these sources intimately; they shaped not only his life but also his apologetics. In works such as *Mere Christianity* and *The Abolition of Man*, Lewis appeals repeatedly—and, some might say, counterintuitively to personal experience as a meaningful source of religious understanding, even as he warned against an exclusive dependence on feeling alone.

In this chapter, I turn to two of Lewis's most influential and decidedly *personal* works to demonstrate the shaping power British Romanticism had on his writings. In *Surprised by Joy* and *A Grief Observed*, Lewis relies on patterns of spiritual autobiography and

---

[9]Congdon, *Journal*, 190.
[10]Congdon, *Journal*, 203.

the conversion narrative to adapt individual experience for public apologetics. In this, he drew on literary techniques from eighteenth- and nineteenth-century life writing to defend and explain Christian faith in the modern world.

Suffocatingly Subjective

Lewis's most prominent autobiographical writing is *Surprised by Joy: The Shape of My Early Life* (1955). By this stage of his career, Lewis was already better known for his work in Christian apologetics than his expertise in medieval and Renaissance literature. Yet Lewis had not set aside his knowledge of language in the creation of his narrative—rather, he builds on this background in the formation of a story that would appeal to readers in his own times.

As has become a habit for me in reading Lewis's works, I find myself drawn to the preface for clues to what he thought he was doing—or, better yet, signs of how he shaped language to form the expectations of his readers. Lewis opens with a plain statement of purpose, explaining his desire to share his spiritual journey and correct some misrepresentations that have begun to appear.[11] Then Lewis makes a series of startling claims—claims that will be familiar to those who have followed my argument in the previous chapter.

First, Lewis suggests that most readers will not find the work of much interest—unless, that is, such an individual has personally experienced what he calls "joy" or an intense desire that cannot be satisfied.[12] For those who have had such an experience, his book will provide a confirmation of that same individual feeling. What one might previously have disregarded as merely an individual idiosyncrasy suddenly appears commonplace. "What! Have *you* felt that too?" Lewis remarks. "I always thought I was the only one."[13]

---

[11]C. S. Lewis, *Surprised by Joy: The Shape of My Early Life* (Boston: Mariner, 2012), vii.
[12]Lewis, *Surprised by Joy*, 17.
[13]Lewis, *Surprised by Joy*, vii.

Next, Lewis identifies his genre explicitly as "the story of my conversion" rather than a more conventional autobiography. The work, he explains, is rather *unlike* those so-called *Confessions* of either Augustine or Rousseau. His story is neither a detailed account of his entire life nor a catalog of beliefs. From one angle, however strange it may sound, Lewis wishes to produce a story that stands on its own, fully apart from his own biography, for he distrusted scholarly interpretations that depended on personal details.[14] The text stands on its own.

Surprised by Joy is certainly personal but also about the sort of "spiritual crisis" that many other readers may have felt. As such, while this is very much his own story, it may simultaneously represent every person's story. Shrewdly, Lewis admits that readers should not expect that he will maintain the exacting standards of modern autobiography, eliminating the need for accuracy in every detail and allowing him the freedom to exclude facts that he would prefer not to share. He wryly asserts, "I do not think there is much loss."[15]

Finally, Lewis makes one of the most startling claims in the entire body of his writings. In a statement so audacious that readers must choose either to ignore it entirely or merely explain it away as the mark of profundity, Lewis appears to undermine the very purpose and genre of his work: "The story is, I fear, suffocatingly subjective."[16] *Suffocatingly subjective?* Surely, this ranks among the most paradoxical declarations in the history of modern autobiography.

Indeed, Lewis has already habituated his readers with a rhetorical gambit. Methodically, as David Jasper observes, Lewis anticipates his critics, for whom the narrative will reek of criminal subjectivity: "Like all good rhetoricians he is always one step

---

[14]In marginal notes to H. W. Garrod's *Wordsworth: Lectures and Essays*, 2nd ed. (Oxford: Clarendon, 1927) (C. S. Lewis Library collection, Wade), Lewis repeatedly complains of biographical interpretation as a kind of gossip that does little to illumine poetics.

[15]Lewis, *Surprised by Joy*, viii

[16]Lewis, *Surprised by Joy*, viii.

ahead."[17] In essence, Lewis suggests that anyone who reads on must already know he speaks truly: this is not about him alone but belongs to the broad experience of humanity. To read on against the grain is to do so without standing. Set in the context of his prior affirmation of a universal, if numinous, longing, Lewis prepares readers to grasp the deep inner logic of his narrative: within all people is a yearning after something more like a dream or a myth than some empirical fact of existence.

Surprised by Joy, as many have noted, was not Lewis's first attempt to publish an autobiographical work. In *The Pilgrim's Regress: An Allegorical Apology for Christianity, Reason and Romanticism* (1933), Lewis narrated his newfound Christian faith in the spirit of John Bunyan's *Pilgrim's Progress*. The book, as he explained a decade later, was a regrettably obscure tale, predicated on an intimate knowledge of his unique philosophical journey through realism, idealism, pantheism, theism, and finally Christianity: "I committed the same sort of blunder as one who should narrate his travels through the Gobi Desert on the assumption that this route was as familiar to the British public as the line from Euston to Crewe."[18]

Yet, just as with *Surprised by Joy*, Lewis aimed to describe a feeling of longing. He denominated this experience "Romanticism" in the subtitle but came to regret the use of the term. In brief, Lewis believed Romanticism suggested too many possible meanings to be helpful ("I now believe it to be a word of such varying senses that it has become useless and should be banished from our vocabulary").[19] But whether Romanticism refers to adventure, the magical/fairy, the Romanesque, the macabre, the egoistic, the revolt against

---

[17]David Jasper, "*The Pilgrim's Regress* and *Surprised by Joy*," in *The Cambridge Companion to C. S. Lewis*, ed. Robert MacSwain and Michael Ward (Cambridge: Cambridge University Press, 2010), 231.

[18]C. S. Lewis, "Afterword to Third Edition," in *The Pilgrim's Regress: An Allegorical Apology for Christianity, Reason and Romanticism*, illustrated by Michael Hague (Grand Rapids, MI: Eerdmans, 1992), 200.

[19]Lewis, "Afterword," 200.

civilization, or an awareness of the natural world, each of these meanings fails to capture what he really felt in discovering Christ.[20] For this reason, Lewis chose to write *The Pilgrim's Regress* in the "disguise" of allegory, for his object was to make his own experience accessible to readers in the form of a story. The intellect cannot grasp such a world. The one thing necessary is imagination.

Romantic Enthusiasm

Imagination may be the linchpin to C. S. Lewis's conversion. To understand why, however, we must look back not only to his English Romantic forebears but to the seminal influence of Methodism on that literary movement. Precisely two hundred years before Lewis grappled with the truth or falsity of Christian faith at Oxford, a coterie of devoted students gathered within the same university in what would emerge as one of the most influential reforming movements in Christianity since the onset of Protestantism.

The Oxford Methodists began as a small group of Anglicans engaged in works of personal and social piety, attending to the sacraments with as much devotion as they showed in caring for the imprisoned and the poor. Their methods, however, were somewhat unusual for members of the Church of England at the time. In fact, the Methodist movement spread through ordained clergy and, more importantly, an itinerant connection of lay preachers who spoke quite literally *outside* churches in open-air events in country fields, cemeteries, and town squares. England at this time faced a rapid transition from agricultural labor to industrial trade, and Methodist societies provided these displaced individuals with a source of social and religious cohesion that others within the Church of England—steeped in its doctrine, traditions, and history—seemed unable (or unwilling) to meet.[21]

---

[20]Lewis, "Afterword," 202.
[21]Jeffrey W. Barbeau, *The Spirit of Methodism: From the Wesleys to a Global Communion* (Downers Grove, IL: IVP Academic, 2019).

Not surprisingly, British Methodists faced stiff opposition to their teachings, despite their steadfast allegiance to the establishment. Among the most frequent and serious charges leveled against them was the claim that these preachers were little more than *enthusiasts*. Far from a term of endearment, the insult insinuated that Methodists engaged in a fanaticism that had both political and spiritual implications. Politically, an enthusiast ran the risk of leading others away from the church into beliefs that undermined the stability of the nation. Spiritually, those denominated enthusiasts allegedly claimed for themselves a kind of inspiration that is only rightly ascribed to the authors of the Bible.

Consider the critique of Methodism introduced by William Warburton, bishop of Gloucester. In *The Doctrine of Grace* (1762), Warburton charges John Wesley and George Whitefield (two of the earliest leaders of the movement) with a mysticism that claims the extraordinary operation of the Holy Spirit akin to the first-century church. Contemporary enthusiasts encourage fanaticism, Warburton alleges, by an overestimation of their own authority: "These men . . . look with admiration on the privileges and powers conferred on those chosen instruments, their imagination grows heated, they forget the difference between the present and the past economy of things, they seem to feel the impressions they hear of, and they assume the airs and mimic the authority of prophets and apostles."[22]

The heart of the problem, for Warburton and other critics, centered on the inward witness of the Spirit that Methodists earnestly taught as a requirement for salvation. Against the commonplace belief that those who had been baptized could rest assured of their salvation or that moral action corroborates belief, revivalists promoted introspective self-awareness as the decisive marker of faith.

---

[22]William Warburton, "The Doctrine of Grace," in *Religion in Romantic England: An Anthology of Primary Sources*, ed. Jeffrey W. Barbeau (Waco, TX: Baylor University Press, 2018), 185.

Influenced by the German Pietist tradition, Methodists encouraged a new heart religion that appealed not only to signs of outward change but to the inward witness that only the Spirit could provide. For John Wesley, the words of the apostle in the epistle to the Romans are a description of what ought to be experienced by all true believers: "The Spirit itself beareth witness with our spirit, that we are the children of God" (Rom 8:16).

When Warburton warns that "their imagination grows heated," he picks up on a wider critique of nonconformist dissent that identified the individual's imagination as the real source of the problem. Imagination was often regarded with suspicion during this time— not as the source of inventive, wondrous worlds that might help us to think about life and truth with greater clarity, but rather the mystifying and potentially misleading haze that obscures reality and darkens the intellect. In the words of English Baptist minister John Foster, "The whole mind may become at length something like a hemisphere of cloud-scenery, filled with an ever-moving train of changing, melting forms, of every color, mingled with rainbows, meteors, and an occasional gleam of pure sunlight."[23]

Not surprisingly, the prosaic association between enthusiasm and Methodism lingered into what we now call the Romantic era. In one of the most inventive compositions of the period—published nearly two decades after John Wesley's death—Leigh Hunt lampooned the Methodist tendency to inflame "the fancies of the impassioned" in a stinging critique of the movement. For Hunt, Methodism translates bodily ailments into spiritual signs of divine providence. The truth lies not in the hand of God but the foolishness of their misguided teaching: "Fever and accidents make the great majority of Methodists. They are converted not by the sunshine but by the

---

[23]John Foster, "On the Application of the Epithet Romantic," in *Essays in a Series of Letters to a Friend* (London: Longman, 1805), 2:11-12; quoted in Barbeau, "Introduction," in *Religion in Romantic England*, xvii.

tempest: stomachaches, rheumatisms, and catarrhs, a constitution destroyed by debauchery and a mind debilitated by ignorance become precious helps to a communion with God."[24]

So, too, for Robert Southey, whose two-volume *The Life of Wesley, and the Rise and Progress of Methodism* (1820) was the first biography of John Wesley penned by an individual who was not a Methodist. Published three decades after Wesley's death, Southey's meticulous study made much of superstition and enthusiasm, highlighting the Wesley family's belief that a ghost ("Old Jeffrey") resided at the Epworth rectory and that many early Methodists reported rapturous, even amorous accounts of their experience of the new birth. In this, Southey extended the popularity of earlier charges of Wesleyan enthusiasm, building on popular portrayals of early Methodism by artists such as William Hogarth in *Credulity, Superstition, and Fanaticism* (1762; see figure 2.3).[25]

There is a tremendous paradox in these attacks. For while some of the most beloved Romantic authors condemned members of the Wesleyan movement, many of those we now associate with Romanticism were accused of propagating religious enthusiasm in their own compositions. Charles Lamb affably referred to William Wordsworth's *The Excursion* as "a kind of 'Natural Methodism,'" and publisher Francis Jeffrey sardonically labeled the same work little more than "the mystical verbiage of the Methodist pulpit," while increasingly the Lake District poets were contemptuously compared to a dissenting sect.[26]

---

[24]Leigh Hunt, "An Attempt to Shew the Folly and Danger of Methodism," in *Religion in Romantic England*, 205.

[25]On Southey's portrayal and the charge of superstition, see Helen Boyles, *Romanticism and Methodism: The Problem of Religious Enthusiasm* (London: Routledge, 2017), 62-72.

[26]Boyles, *Romanticism and Methodism*, 1-2, 7; cf. Frederick C. Gill, *The Romantic Movement and Methodism: A Study of English Romanticism and the Evangelical Revival* (London: Epworth, 1937), and Jasper Cragwall, *Lake Methodism: Polite Literature and Popular Religion, 1780–1830* (Columbus: Ohio State University Press, 2013).

Figure 2.3. William Hogarth, *Credulity, Superstition, and Fanaticism* (1762)

Indeed, while each criticized John Wesley for his alleged excesses, the Lake poets were all intimately familiar with Methodist teachings and ministry. William Wordsworth almost certainly heard John Wesley preach in Cockermouth, Cumbria, where Wesley preached five times when Wordsworth lived along the main

street as a boy (1770–1778).[27] Memorably, Robert Southey once met
Wesley in what Helen Boyles describes as a "chance encounter" in
which Wesley, emerging from his lodging at Bath, happened upon
the six-year old-child and, "struck by his appearance," proceeded
solemnly to place "his hands on Southey's head" and bless him.[28]
And Samuel Taylor Coleridge thought so highly of Southey's
massive study that he kept a copy of the book at his bedside, writing
voluminous marginalia that describe how the biography had continued to challenge him in times of turmoil: "How many and many
an hour of Self-oblivion do I owe to this Life of Wesley—how often
have I argued with it, questioned, remonstrated, been peevish &
asked pardon—then again listened, & cried, Right! Excellent!"[29]

ROMANTIC LIFE WRITING

C. S. Lewis was certainly familiar with Methodism and the legacy
of eighteenth-century enthusiasm when he composed his own
autobiographical works. Indeed, there are vivid signs of Wesleyan
theology throughout his writings, which ought not surprise us.
Lewis was, of course, an Anglican, and there are few greater Anglicans in recent memory than John Wesley. I, for one, have always
had a suspicion that Eustace Scrubb in the Chronicles of Narnia
was portrayed broadly in the guise of a twentieth-century British
Methodist. In *The Voyage of the Dawn Treader*, Eustace is introduced as a child from "very up-to-date and advanced people" who
don't smoke, drink, or fight in wars.[30] And is there any more

---

[27]Boyles, *Romanticism and Methodism*, 82.
[28]Boyles, *Romanticism and Methodism*, 61.
[29]Samuel Taylor Coleridge, *Marginalia*, ed. H. J. Jackson and George Whalley, 6 parts, vol.
  12 of *The Collected Works of Samuel Taylor Coleridge* (Princeton, NJ: Princeton University Press, 2000), 5:121.
[30]C. S. Lewis, *The Voyage of the Dawn Treader* (New York: HarperCollins, 1994), 3. Notably, Lewis had his addresses for *Mere Christianity* checked in advance by, among others,
  a British Methodist (C. S. Lewis, "Preface," *Mere Christianity* [New York: HarperOne,
  2000], xi).

Wesleyan image of new birth in the Chronicles than the portrayal of Eustace's dragon skin peeled off and washed away later in the story? This, of course, is little more than speculation.

What is certain is that Methodist practices of life writing shaped modern autobiography, beginning in the Romantic period and continuing throughout the nineteenth century. Early Methodist narratives show signs of Puritan influence, in which the gradual realization of salvation unfolds in a series of stages from initial grace in the knowledge of the law, to faith tested by doubt and despair, until final repentance and assurance of divine pardon.[31] But Methodist practices of journaling and diary keeping added another twist to earlier literary conventions. Inspired by the guidance of their mother, Susanna, as well as Jeremy Taylor's *Holy Living* and *Holy Dying*, John and Charles Wesley each maintained diaries to track the state of their souls throughout the day. John Wesley then used these detailed records to compose longer prose journals, sometimes written months or years after the original events. This practice allowed Wesley to shape personal experiences into apologetic narratives, "with the benefit of hindsight, especially in response to attacks upon his character and reputation."[32]

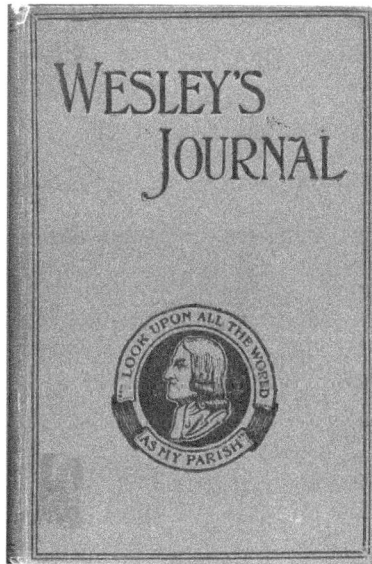

Figure 2.4. C. S. Lewis's personal copy of *John Wesley's Journal*

[31]D. Bruce Hindmarsh, *The Evangelical Conversion Narrative: Spiritual Autobiography in Early Modern England* (Oxford: Oxford University Press, 2005), 36-37.

[32]Vicki Tolar Burton, *Spiritual Literacy in John Wesley's Methodism: Reading, Writing, and Speaking to Believe* (Waco, TX: Baylor University Press, 2008), 78.

Lewis's personal library includes a hardbound copy of *John Wesley's Journal*. The volume has Lewis's signature at the front, numerous underlined passages, and even some corrections to typographical errors at various points within the text. Alongside the editor's remark that Wesley frequently preached more than five thousand sermons annually, Lewis notes in astonishment that such a practice would amount to more than a dozen sermons a day![33] Significantly, Lewis's marginalia inside Wesley's *Journal* indicate that he completed reading the volume in October 1960, only months after the death of his wife, Joy Davidman, and around the same time he wrote *A Grief Observed*.

Unquestionably, *A Grief Observed* is among C. S. Lewis's most beloved works. I agree: *A Grief Observed* grabbed hold of me as few other books when I first read it as an undergraduate. The narrative of raw turmoil over faith and doubt in the midst of intense personal suffering made me feel as though I had entered the most private and sacred spaces of a man's life. The back cover of my first copy set the stage for just such a reading:

> In April 1956, C. S. Lewis, a confirmed bachelor, married Joy Davidman, an American poet with two small children. After four brief, intensely happy years, Lewis found himself alone again, and inconsolable. To defend himself against the loss of belief in God, Lewis wrote this journal, an eloquent statement of rediscovered faith. In it he freely confesses his doubts, his rage, and his awareness of human frailty. In it he finds again the way back to life.[34]

Indeed, I have observed much of the same appreciation for Lewis's willingness to engage in profoundly personal disclosure among my students, who read the book just as I did decades ago.

---

[33] See C. S. Lewis marginalia in John Wesley, *John Wesley's Journal* (London: Isbister, 1902), xiv (C. S. Lewis Library collection, Wade).

[34] Rear cover advertisement, *A Grief Observed*, by C. S. Lewis, Afterword by Chad Walsh (New York: Bantam, 1976).

Yet some have questioned whether the work ought to be read as a personal memoir. As many know, Lewis first published *A Grief Observed* under the pseudonym "N. W. Clerk." Michael Ward, for his part, refers to the book only under Clerk's name to reflect "the pseudonymous nature of the book that was actually published in 1961."[35] Most believe that Lewis, ever guarding against the personal heresy, simply wished to avoid encouraging his readership to interpret his writings by way of biography. According to this view, rather than putting his private suffering out into the public domain, Lewis sought to share his lament discreetly without broadcasting his personal life to the world.

Others contend that Lewis wrote pseudonymously to provide an "everyman" account of grief. Walter Hooper set the stage for such a reading by interpreting the work as "less the expression of raw agony and more as a rhetorical construct intended to help others through the process of grief."[36] Building on Hooper's assertion, George Musacchio offers a more startling argument along the same trajectory, suggesting that Lewis never struggled with his faith in the months after Davidman's death at all. Contrary to such a reading, Musacchio appeals to personal correspondence by Lewis and concludes, "Joy's death hurt her husband deeply, but it did not shatter his view of God; it did not make his world collapse around him; it did not vitiate his literary talent."[37]

While I think it would be foolish to ignore the personal dimension of Lewis's writing on grief—for only days after her passing, he mused, "I can't describe the apparent unreality of my life. . . . I'm like a sleep-walker at the moment"[38]—we have good reason to believe that Lewis

---

[35]Michael Ward, "On Suffering," in MacSwain and Ward, *Cambridge Companion*, 214.

[36]Walter Hooper, *Through Joy and Beyond: A Pictorial Biography of C. S. Lewis* (New York: Macmillan, 1982), 151.

[37]George Musacchio, "Fiction in *A Grief Observed*," *VII: An Anglo-American Literary Review* 8 (1987): 81.

[38]*CLCSL* 3 1171 (July 15, 1960). For more on Lewis's rhetoric, see David C. Downing, "A Grief Obscured: C. S. Lewis on Sorrow and Hope," in *Persona and Paradox: Issues of*

fashioned *A Grief Observed* according to earlier models of journal writing in the eighteenth and nineteenth centuries. Just as Wesley wrote his *Journal* as if the inward affairs of his spiritual life were poured directly onto the page, wholly unmediated, so Lewis constructs a narrative identity as if he has only just scrawled his thoughts on a series of blank notebooks found lying around his house.

The first effort to convince readers that *A Grief Observed* originates in a series of scrawled diaries appears at the start of chapter two: "For the first time I have looked back and read these notes. They appall me."[39] In the same chapter, the narrator describes rereading his thoughts on the page: "I wrote that last night. It was a yell rather than a thought. Let me try that over again."[40] The final chapter confirms the reader's earlier impression as the narrator brings his argument to a close: "This is the fourth—and the last—empty MS. book I can find in the house; at least nearly empty, for there are some pages of very ancient arithmetic at the end by J."[41] Here, the occasional nature of the narrator's writing is interrupted by the alleged lack of commonplace notebooks. He could go no further. He could not continue.

Singling out these rhetorical markers brings the constructed nature of Lewis's *A Grief Observed* to the fore. This is no mere memoir of random facts about a life but a careful narrative with a clear beginning, middle, and end. In fact, if readers haven't picked up on his point by the fourth chapter, Lewis's narrator is keen to let everyone in on the secret, explaining the order of these chapters in a revealing look at the interior logic of the whole. Indeed, he's so overt that readers may be unwilling to allow him to break the spell. Rather than a series of random notebook jottings in a gradual

---

Identity for C. S. Lewis, His Friends and Associates, ed. Suzanne Bray and William Gray (Newcastle upon Tyne: Cambridge Scholars, 2012), 37-48.

[39]C. S. Lewis, *A Grief Observed* (New York: HarperCollins, 2000), 17.

[40]Lewis, *Grief Observed*, 30.

[41]Lewis, *Grief Observed*, 59. "J" appears to represent the narrator's child.

movement through stages of grief, Lewis discloses the three preceding rhetorical movements in the book: "The notes have been
about myself, about H., and about God."[42] Put differently, Lewis
explains that his book divides into four separate parts:

1. The feelings of grief for the individual self (chapter one)
2. The feelings of loss related to the one who is grieved (chapter two)
3. The narrator's private struggle with God (chapter three)
4. A final resolution to the whole (chapter four)

Lewis's achievement in *A Grief Observed* is remarkable: his readers
refuse to give up the suspension of disbelief even after he tells them
what he's doing. This is the art in his apologetic.

In selecting the illusion of a notebook or spiritual journal in the
composition of his thoughts on grief, Lewis picked up on a Methodist practice that shaped Romantic England at the end of the eighteenth and early nineteenth centuries. Journals were among the
foremost means for an author to testify to the interior work of the
Spirit. Unlike biographical works written by or about great political
or economic figures, journals elevated the voices of ordinary men
and women. They could be shared in networks among friends, read
aloud for mutual edification, and maintained in private hands to
allow authors (especially women) to maintain control of their own
authorial voices.[43] In fact, as I have already stated, Lewis's personal
library confirms that he was reading Wesley's *Journal* around this
same time (only months after Joy's death), and pseudonymous au-
thorship allowed Lewis greater freedom to fashion a character that
flowed over the boundaries of strictly personal experience.

---

[42]Lewis, *Grief Observed*, 62.

[43]Andrew O. Winckles, *Eighteenth-Century Women's Writing and the Methodist Media Revolution: "Consider the Lord as Ever Present Reader"* (Liverpool: Liverpool University Press, 2019), 50, 64-67.

ROMANTIC AUTOBIOGRAPHY

While journaling became an increasingly familiar mode of life writing during the Romantic period, conversion narratives and various other forms of personal writing continued to be popular. Alongside these works, however, is a notable rise in the concept of autobiography. In fact, the English word first appeared in the Romantic period: William Taylor initially coined the term in 1797 to describe "self-biography," and in 1809, Robert Southey refers to "autobiography" in an article appearing in the *Quarterly Review*.[44] These early uses of the term allude to a sense of self-mastery, authority, and universality in writing about one's life for the benefit of readers.

The new Romantic sense of autobiographical self-understanding is already present in developments within the conversion narrative genre. Among the most well-known spiritual autobiographies in the period was Thomas Scott's *The Force of Truth* (1779), a work that recorded his transformation not from a vile sinner to a newborn saint but his intellectual progress from rationalist Socinianism (the immediate precursor to Unitarianism) to historically orthodox trinitarianism. The problem is not so much wrong *actions*—say gambling, drinking, or dueling—the real issue is wrong *thinking*.

Yet, in what amounts to further evidence that any appeal to inward feeling risked accusations of enthusiasm, Scott takes care repeatedly to distance himself from the scandalous charge of Methodism: "I acted not in the character of an inquirer, but in full confidence that I was pleading the cause of truth, and had no more thought of becoming what the world calls a Methodist, than of turning Mahometan."[45] Nevertheless, Scott defends the movement as "in opinion and practice entirely free from Enthusiasm," even if "the enemy will be sure to scatter his tares" wherever "the Lord sows

---

[44]"Autobiography, n," Oxford English Dictionary Online, Oxford University Press, 2022.
[45]Thomas Scott, *The Force of Truth: An Authentic Narrative* (London, 1779), 171.

his good seed."[46] John Henry Newman (one of Lewis's favorite authors) felt so indebted to the work that he claimed Scott was "the writer who made a deeper impression on my mind than any other, and to whom (humanly speaking) I almost owe my soul."[47]

In fact, Scott's *Force of Truth* may well have influenced one of Lewis's most famous lines. For just as Lewis compares Christianity to the rising of the sun, "not only because I see it, but because by it I see everything else,"[48] so too Scott defends his own experience of faith as beyond the conventional wisdom of this world. He begins by asserting his own felt experience: "Since that season every thing I have experienced in my own heart, every thing I have heard and read, every thing I observe around me, confirms and establishes me in the assured belief of those truths which I have received." Scott then compares his own faith to the light of the sun: "nor do I . . . any more doubt their being from God, than I doubt whether the sun shines, when I see its light, and am warmed with its refreshing beams. I see the powerful effects of them continually amongst those to whom I preach; I experience the power of them daily in my own soul."[49] While there is presently no record that confirms that Lewis had read *The Force of Truth*, Scott's writing signaled an important shift in spiritual autobiography and subsequent forms of Romantic-era life writing alike.

These "enthusiastic" origins of Romantic autobiography are particularly relevant to C. S. Lewis, especially in the influence of William Wordsworth on his most personal writings. Many readers will recognize that Lewis derives the title of his own conversion narrative from Wordsworth's famous sonnet:

---

[46]Scott, *Force of Truth*, 201.

[47]John Henry Newman, *Apologia pro Vita Sua* (London: Penguin, 1994), 26. Copies of Newman's works, often heavily annotated, appear in Lewis's personal library at the Wade.

[48]C. S. Lewis, "Is Theology Poetry?," in *The Weight of Glory and Other Addresses* (New York: HarperOne, 2001), 140.

[49]Scott, *Force of Truth*, 142.

SURPRIZED by joy—impatient as the Wind
I wished to share the transport—Oh! with whom
But Thee, long buried in the silent Tomb,
That spot which no vicissitude can find?
Love, faithful love recalled thee to my mind—
But how could I forget thee?—Through what power,
Even for the least division of an hour,
Have I been so beguiled as to be blind
To my most grievous loss!—That thought's return
Was the worst pang that sorrow ever bore,
Save one, one only, when I stood forlorn,
Knowing my heart's best treasure was no more;
That neither present time, nor years unborn
Could to my sight that heavenly face restore.[50]

The circumstances of the poem—the death of Wordsworth's daughter Caroline—give a melancholy character to the whole. This is not joy abundant in a celebration of life but the awareness of profound grief after a moment of forgetfulness. Memory paused for only a second leads to self-doubt and despair: "How could I forget thee?" This leads to "the worst pang that sorrow ever bore," except in the first moment of realized loss.

Lewis's conversion narrative certainly resembles Wordsworth's poem, with its measured grief and longing. Just as Wordsworth's poem focuses on death as a moment of existential crisis, so Lewis's opening chapter pivots on the death of his mother. He laments that this was "my first religious experience."[51] Immediately following his definition of joy as desire and longing, Lewis explains that, with his mother's death, all tranquility disappeared from his life:

---

[50]William Wordsworth, "Surprized by Joy—Impatient as the Wind," in *Wordsworth's Poetry and Prose*, Norton critical ed., ed. Nicholas Halmi (New York: Norton, 2014), 528.
[51]Lewis, *Surprised by Joy*, 20.

"There was to be much fun, many pleasures, many stabs of Joy; but no more of the old security. It was sea and islands now; the great continent had sunk like Atlantis."[52] Still, Lewis surprisingly disclaimed the connection to Wordsworth. To one correspondent, he wrote, "I don't think it matters whether the title suggests Wordsworth or not."[53]

Instead of relating a series of immoral actions from which he was delivered, Lewis's *Surprised by Joy* conveys the growth of his mind. He reveals the early children's literature that stimulated his imagination, the painful loneliness of boarding school, and the gradual awakening of his heart through friendships and reading. Throughout it all, the story revolves around his interior life far more than the outward characters of the narrative: abusive schoolmates, life and death in wartime, and unspoken indiscretions never take center stage spiritually. In this, subsequent demurs aside, Lewis highlights the same features of Romanticism to which he had previously aspired in *The Pilgrim's Regress*. For just as *Surprised by Joy* shows how "joy" names the deepest desires of Lewis's heart—the signposts pointing beyond himself to the divine—so in *The Pilgrim's Regress* Lewis directs readers to the longing that cannot be satisfied by any material objects in this life.

Another possibility exists. Perhaps the allusion to Wordsworth depends less on the title of the poem as the poet himself and, by implication, his great autobiography: *The Prelude* (1805). As I explained in the first chapter, Lewis read Wordsworth's long poem and reported to his friend Arthur Greeves that he began slowly to admire it. Early on, Lewis is rather pompous: "as bad as a poem could be in some ways" yet intermixed with remarkable passages throughout.[54]

---

[52]Lewis, *Surprised by Joy*, 21.
[53]Lewis added that it would be appropriate to advertise the work as a conversion narrative on the back cover (*CLCSL* 3.614 [June 1, 1955]).
[54]*CLCSL* 1.468 (October 18, 1919). Elsewhere Lewis claims his own poetic achievement will make Wordsworth's *Prelude* look comparably juvenile (*CLCSL* 2.55 [March 16, 1932]).

THE PRELUDE,

GROWTH OF A POET'S MIND;

AN AUTOBIOGRAPHICAL POEM;

WILLIAM WORDSWORTH.

LONDON:
EDWARD MOXON, DOVER STREET.
1850.

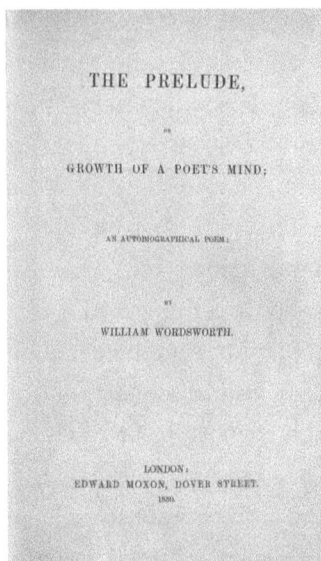

Figure 2.5. *The Prelude* by William Wordsworth

In later years, however, Lewis read and reread *The Prelude* many times. He describes the reading experience as one constantly nourishing his soul, reporting to one correspondent that it is "Always just a little better than one remembers from the last reading, I think."[55] Only a few years before writing *Surprised by Joy*, Lewis reported that *The Prelude* had been one of only two poetic works that remained with him throughout his entire spiritual pilgrimage.[56]

What did Wordsworth's long poem provide Lewis? At minimum, a spiritual vision of ordinary life paired with a poetic achievement that he respected. Yet, while *The Prelude* does not exude the sort of overt religiosity that most conversion narratives aim to illumine, the poem displays many of the same characteristics, even when it subverts them.[57] As with Scott before him, and Lewis later, Wordsworth emphasizes not outward acts of individual sin but inward states of mind that gradually reveal the growth of his mind.

To take but one familiar example, consider Wordsworth's well-known childhood experience of stealing a boat and rowing away from shore. The event leads not to reflection on his own sinfulness—as it did with Augustine's pear-stealing—but an awakening of consciousness. The boy loosens the boat and perceives a cliff beyond

---

[55]*CLCSL* 2.764 (February 12, 1947).
[56]*CLCSL* 3.111 (April 23, 1951).
[57]I have described the poem in further detail in Jeffrey W. Barbeau, "Romantic Religion, Life Writing, and Conversion Narratives," *The Wordsworth Circle* 47 (2016): 32-39.

the edge of the water that leaves him silent and trembling. Yet Wordsworth's encounter with nature only defers his longing for assurance: this is neither a moment of despair nor a mark of conversion but a "spot of time"—a "visionary gleam," as he calls such an encounter in his "Ode: Intimations of Immortality"—that nourishes his soul on a journey of discovery.[58] Indeed, in what many deem a tribute to Augustine's *Confessions* before him, Word-

Figure 2.6. Benjamin Robert Haydon, *William Wordsworth on Helvellyn* (1842)

sworth's thirteen-book *Prelude* concludes with reconciliation in the experience of grace that leads to freedom: "Oh, who is he that hath his whole life long / Preserved, enlarged, this freedom in himself?— / For this alone is greater liberty" (13:120-22).

For his part, Lewis draws back at the end. At the conclusion of *Surprised by Joy*, Lewis explains that his interest in "joy" has almost entirely lost its luster: "I cannot, indeed, complain, like Wordsworth, that the visionary gleam has passed away. . . . Not, of course, that I don't often catch myself stopping to stare at roadside objects of even less importance."[59]

RESTLESS INQUIRY

Lewis's spiritual pilgrimage owes much to the British Romantics. Wordsworth's poetry helped him to articulate an experience of

---

[58]Cf. William Wordsworth, "Ode: Intimations of Immortality," line 56, in *Wordsworth's Poetry and Prose*, 435; cf. Graham Davidson, *The Intelligible Ode: Intimations of Paradise* (Cambridge: Lutterworth, 2023)

[59]Lewis, *Surprised by Joy*, 238.

desire, longing, or "joy" in verses that Lewis returned to repeatedly throughout life. Alongside Wordsworth's poetry, however, was another companion that has gone almost entirely unrecognized in studies of Lewis's life writing: Samuel Taylor Coleridge.[60]

Much as with Wordsworth's poetry, we know that Lewis encountered Coleridge's poetry early on. Unlike Wordsworth, however, Coleridge is better known for his philosophical and theological prose. Often discursive, Coleridge had a reputation for circling around subjects with dizzying depth. His reputation for talking was such that we even find Lewis making a humorous reference to Coleridge after listening to his aunt rattle on uninterruptedly during a visit in the early 1920s. She is "like an old drawer, full of both rubbish and valuable things, but all thrown together in great disorder," Lewis claims. During their time together, his aunt pontificated on women's suffrage, heroism, existence, the material world, ectoplasm, Plato and Bolshevism, the words of Christ, Pekinese dogs, and the existence of God. He concludes his account with affectionate fatigue, "I imagine a morning with Coleridge must have been something like this."[61]

Stories such as this demonstrate Lewis's awareness of the lore that surrounds early Romantic collaborators such as Coleridge and Wordsworth, but there is a deeper philosophical and theological debt that such an account might betray. In fact, even in his

---

[60]In the most extensive study of Lewis and Romanticism, the authors consider Coleridge more a prop than a source, attributing his apparent influence to a common philosophical tradition rather than a direct literary debt. The authors even dismiss the potential Coleridgean link to Barfield: "If we can trace any clear influence on Lewis from Wordsworth or Coleridge, it most likely takes the form of *indirect* influence through the good offices of George MacDonald" (James Prothero and Donald T. Williams, *Gaining a Face: The Romanticism of C. S. Lewis* [Newcastle upon Tyne: Cambridge Scholars Publishing, 2013], 20-22). More helpful, in this respect, is the excellent survey by Wayne Martindale, "Romantics," in *Reading the Classics with C. S. Lewis*, ed. Thomas L. Martin (Grand Rapids, MI: Baker, 2000), 203-26.

[61]The conversation was with Lily Suffern (1860–1934), Lewis's mother's sister (see C. S. Lewis, *All My Road Before Me: The Diary of C. S. Lewis, 1922-1927*, ed. Walter Hooper [San Diego: Harcourt Brace Jovanovich, 1991], 127-28).

discussion of Romanticism in *The Pilgrim's Regress* we find Lewis referring to the beginning of Coleridge's "Kubla Khan" as that "unnamable something" he had been trying to describe.[62] In Coleridge, Lewis found a writer who had traveled a similar spiritual journey, a thinker who had come to reject materialism for trinitarian faith. In fact, Lewis's personal diaries, correspondence, and marginalia reveal that he came under Coleridge's influence at a decisive moment in his life—just as he was facing his stoutest questions about belief and unbelief in the late 1920s.

The first book that caught his attention was Coleridge's autobiographical masterpiece, *Biographia Literaria* (1817). A disparate work of life writing, aesthetics, and literary criticism all bound together, Coleridge's *Biographia Literaria* is best known for producing one of the most influential theories of the imagination in modern thought. If Lewis's personal diary and letters are any indication, we can confidently say that Lewis took Coleridge's *Biographia* very seriously indeed. In 1927 he thought carefully about the book, marking in multiple diary entries that he was wrestling over Coleridge's famous definition of imagination. In January, he describes his situation as an "unholy muddle" in which various schools of thought all vied for ascendency in his mind: bits of anthroposophy, psychoanalysis, idealism, and rationalism all pressing into one another; meanwhile, there was still "the danger of falling back into most childish superstitions, or of running into dogmatic materialism."[63] Once again, he found solace the following day in Wordsworth, comforting his endlessly restless heart.[64]

Yet, however reassuring his studies made him, by April of the same year, Lewis was still thinking about the imagination, and it's clear that Coleridge was still very much on his mind. In a letter to

---

[62]Lewis, *Pilgrim's Regress*, 204.
[63]Lewis, *All My Road*, 431-32 (January 18, 1927).
[64]Lewis, *All My Road*, 432 (January 19, 1927).

his brother Warren, Lewis writes at length about the *Biographia*. While the book is too philosophical for his brother's taste, Lewis thinks he would like the account of the charity school Christ's Hospital under James Bowyer (as something of a complement to Charles Lamb's narrative of the same), as well as Coleridge's literary criticism more generally. The finest part, he thinks, is what Lewis deems perhaps "the best unconscious bit of literary joke that was ever played."[65] He then proceeds to explain the twisted route Coleridge takes in making the distinction between imagination and fancy, through sideroads in Spinoza, Kant, and a host of distractions that all conclude with a less than satisfying resolution: "'And what good came of it at last, quoth little Peterkin.' The answer is *nothing*—nothing whatsoever."[66]

Lewis may have been exasperated, but he certainly wasn't the first to read, reread, and finally leave Coleridge's *Biographia* with a mixture of disorientation and appreciation. Nevertheless, we still find him discussing the *Biographia* in subsequent years, referring to Coleridge's headmaster in a letter to one correspondent and quoting from the text in a later letter to Dorothy Sayers.[67] What's more, the *Biographia* may have shaped some of the vexing choices Lewis made in devising the plot of *Surprised by Joy*. While the *Biographia* lacks the clear narrative arc that Lewis's conversion story offers, both detail their educational formation and a change of mind from early Christian upbringing, through periods of doubt, to faith in Christ.

Around this time, Lewis also began to study another work by Coleridge: *The Friend*. Lewis's personal library includes a heavily inscribed copy: a striking edition from Bohn's Standard Library. Lewis's copy stands out in his personal library for containing not

---

[65]*CLCSL* 1.685 (April 18, 1927).
[66]*CLCSL* 1.685-86 (April 18, 1927). The very next paragraph begins, "It reminds me of my friend Barfield . . ."
[67]*CLCSL* 3.570 (February 27, 1955, to Martyn Skinner); 3.860 (June 25, 1957).

only a list of beneficial passages opposite the table of contents but also a handwritten index that Lewis has added at the back of the volume.[68] His marginalia detail more than thirty different categories, singling out central concepts in Coleridge's thought, including Babel, biographies, dreams, duty, faith, feeling, genius, man, nature, Plato, perception, pragmatism, and "rambling talkers." He also includes extensive biographical material in an entry devoted to Coleridge's life and thought:

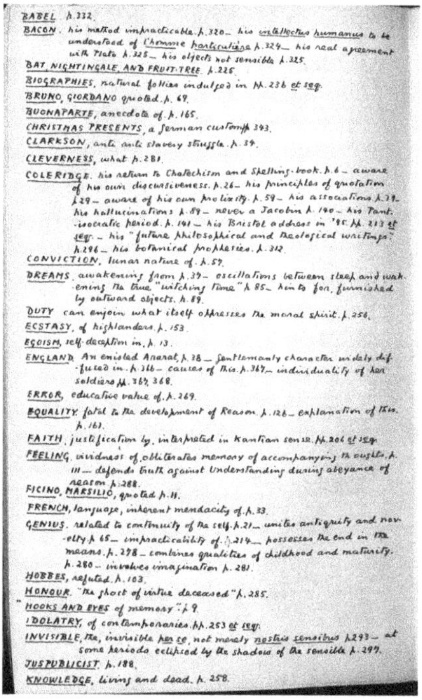

BABEL p. 332.
BACON. his method impracticable. p. 320— his intellectus humanus to be understood of l'homme particulière p. 324— his real agreement with Plato p. 325— his objects not sensible p. 325.
BAT, NIGHTINGALE, AND FRUIT-TREE p. 225.
BIOGRAPHIES, natural follies indulged in pp. 236 et seq.
BRUNO, GIORDANO quoted. p. 69.
BUONAPARTE, anecdote of. p. 165.
CHRISTMAS PRESENTS, a German custom p 343.
CLARKSON, anti anti slavery struggle. p. 34.
CLEVERNESS, what p. 281.
COLERIDGE. his return to Chatechism and Spelling-book. p. 6— aware of his own discursiveness. p. 26— his principles of quotation p 29— aware of his own prolixity. p. 59— his associations p. 79— his hallucinations p. 89— never a Jacobin p. 140— his Pantisocratic period. p. 141— his Bristol address in '95. pp. 213 et seq.— his "future philosophical and theological writings." p. 296— his botanical prophesies. p. 312.
CONVICTION, lunar nature of. p. 57.
DREAMS. awakening from p. 37— oscillations between sleep and wakening the true "witching time" p 85— hints for, furnished by outward objects. p. 89.
DUTY can enjoin what itself oppresses the moral spirit. p. 256.
ECSTASY, of highlanders. p. 153.
EGOISM, self-deception in, p. 13.
ENGLAND An enisled Ararat, p. 38— gentlemanly character widely diffused in. p 366— causes of this. p. 367— individuality of her soldiers pp. 367, 368.
ERROR, educative value of. p. 269.
EQUALITY fatal to the development of Reason. p. 126— explanation of this. p. 161.
FAITH. justification by. interpreted in Kantian sense. pp. 206 et seq.
FEELING. vividness of. obliterates memory of accompanying thoughts. p. 111— defends truth against Understanding during abeyance of reason p. 288.
FICINO, MARSILIO, quoted p. 11.
FRENCH, language, inherent mendacity of. p. 33.
GENIUS. related to continuity of the self. p. 21— unites antiquity and novelty p 65— impracticability of. p. 214— possesses the end in the means. p. 278— combines qualities of childhood and maturity. p. 280— involves imagination p. 281.
HOBBES, refuted. p. 103.
HONOUR. "the ghost of virtue deceased" p. 285.
"HOOKS AND EYES of memory" p 9.
IDOLATRY, of contemporaries. pp. 253 et seq.
INVISIBLE, the, invisible per se, not merely nostris sensibus p293— at some periods eclipsed by the shadow of the sensible p. 297.
JUSPUBLICIST. p. 188.
KNOWLEDGE, living and dead. p. 258.

Figure 2.7. Marginalia by C. S. Lewis in S. T. Coleridge, *The Friend: A Series of Essays*

COLERIDGE. His return to Chatechism [*sic*] and Spelling-book, p. 6—aware of his own discursiveness. p. 26—his principles of quotation p. 29—aware of his own prolixity. p. 59—his associations p. 79—his hallucinations p. 89—never a Jacobin p 140—his Pantisocratic period. p. 141—his Bristol address in '95. pp. 213 et seq—his "future philosophical and theological writings." p. 296—his botanical prophesies. p. 312.

Lewis even notes the pivotal Coleridgean distinction between Reason and Understanding, which differentiates intuited spiritual knowledge

[68]Marginalia by C. S. Lewis in Samuel Taylor Coleridge, *The Friend: A Series of Essays* (London: Bell & Daldy, 1865), [p. 386] and verso of p. 389 (C. S. Lewis Library collection, Wade).

from sensory intellection—the distinction may well point to what Lewis means when he appeals to inward feeling or knowledge of the heart. I suggest that Coleridge plays a more significant role in Lewis's conversion than scholars have heretofore recognized.

Figure 2.8. C. S. Lewis at Stonehenge, April 8, 1925

THE CONVERSION OF C. S. LEWIS

The significance of reading Coleridge in early 1929 becomes clearer if we remember how Lewis explained his conversion to theism and, eventually, Christianity in *Surprised by Joy*: "In the Trinity Term of 1929 I gave in, and admitted that God was God, and knelt and prayed: perhaps, that night, the most dejected and reluctant convert in all England."[69] Alister Mc-Grath has confidently challenged Lewis's self-avowed timeline of events, stating, "In preparing for this biography, I read all of Lewis's published works in their order of composition. At no point in Lewis's writings of 1929 did I discern any signs of the dramatic developments that he describes as having taken place in his inner life that year. There is no hint of a change in tone or tempo in any works written up to January 1930."[70] While scholars have questioned Lewis's dating of the event—rightly so, for it appears that his turn from atheism to theism was complete by the middle of 1930—the facile dismissal of events in 1929 ignores the

---

[69]Lewis, *Surprised by Joy*, 228-29. Trinity term was between April 28 and June 22, 1929.
[70]Alister McGrath, *C. S. Lewis—A Life: Eccentric Genius, Reluctant Prophet* (Carol Stream, IL: Tyndale, 2013), 141.

significance of that period in his intellectual journey.[71] What if the change Lewis experienced in his inner life—his gradual conversion from atheism to theism—cannot be found in the published writings but only in the marks and annotations of the books he read?

Here we must take what at first glance appears to be a sharp detour: Lewis's friendship with Owen Barfield and Alan Richard Griffiths. Barfield was undoubtedly a significant figure in Lewis's life, and, indeed, Lewis ranks Barfield alongside Arthur Greeves as among the most important contributors to his eventual conversion to Christianity.[72] Much has been made of the so-called great war between Lewis and Barfield, but less well known is Griffiths, who often receives only a passing mention in biographies of Lewis. Yet the presence of Coleridge ties these three men together in a rather extraordinary and previously unrecognized way.[73]

The Lewis-Griffiths relationship is of no small importance during these years, as Lewis quickly transitioned from tutor, to mentor, to friend. In fact, at Lewis's recommendation, Griffiths began to read Coleridge and found his life suddenly and irrevocably changed, describing the illuminating experience years later in his memoir, *The Golden String* (1954) (a presentation copy inscribed by the author, reading, "In memory of twenty-five years of friendship," may still be found in Lewis's personal library).[74] The little-known story bears recounting in some detail.

---

[71]The tendency to focus on a single moment in Lewis's conversion story is deeply problematic; his conversion ought, I think, be regarded as a *series* of conversions. For a fuller account of Lewis's long religious and philosophical journey, see Norbert Feinendegen's detailed account of the chronology in "The Philosopher's Progress: C. S. Lewis' Intellectual Journey from Atheism to Theism," *Journal of Inklings Studies* 8 (2018): 103-43; cf. Feinendegen, *C. S. Lewis: Überrascht von Gott: Wie der große christliche Denker zum Glauben fand* (Münster: Verlag, 2023).

[72]*CLCSL* 1.969 (September 22, 1931).

[73]Norbert Feinendegen and Arend Smilde, eds., *The "Great War" of Owen Barfield and C. S. Lewis: Philosophical Writings, 1927–1930*, Inklings Studies Supplements 1 (Edinburgh: Edinburgh University Press, 2015).

[74][Dom] Bede Griffiths, *The Golden String* (New York: P. J. Kenedy and Sons, 1954) (C. S. Lewis Library collection, Wade). The inscription from the presentation copy in the Wade Center is from the Harvill Press edition of 1954.

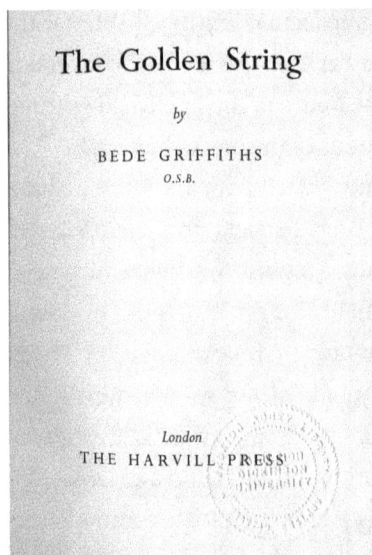

Figure 2.9. *The Golden String* by Bede Griffiths

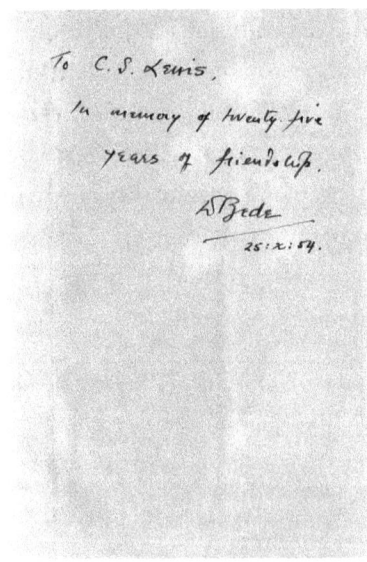

Figure 2.10. Bede Griffiths's inscription to
C. S. Lewis in *The Golden String* (1954)

After finishing at Oxford in 1925, Griffiths followed Lewis's advice to work through many of the "Greats" of philosophy as a supplement to his undergraduate education. Lewis had "the most exact and penetrating mind I had ever encountered," Griffiths explains, and so his reading in philosophy was accompanied by regular correspondence with him.[75] From Griffith's point of view, the two men journeyed together on something of a spiritual quest: "It was through him that my mind was gradually brought back to Christianity. During the following years we pursued the study of Christianity together, and first one of us and then the other would make the discovery of some masterpiece of Christian thought which we had not known before. . . . An unseen hand seemed to be leading us both to the same goal."[76] Griffiths read Descartes, Spinoza, Berkeley, and others, but it was Coleridge that seems

[75]Griffiths, *Golden String*, 44.
[76]Griffiths, *Golden String*, 44.

to have changed the landscape of his life: "In this I was helped by reading two books by Coleridge, which Lewis recommended to me at this time, the *Aids to Reflection* and *The Friend*. These books are not very widely read, but they are the work of one of the most universal minds in English literature, written at the end of his life when he had mastered all the new German philosophy and created a new synthesis from it."[77]

Prompted by Lewis's recommendation, Griffiths gained two insights from Coleridge: (1) he was a "great thinker who employed all his powers as a philosopher in defence of orthodox Christianity," and (2) he developed a "synthesis between the philosophy of Kant and that Platonic philosophy" to which he had been attracted from his "earliest years."[78] Griffiths was finally able to make sense of the relationship between phenomena and the "'idea' which is the source of its reality." Reading Coleridge—especially the *Biographia Literaria* on imagination, *Aids to Reflection* on religious language, and *The Friend* on human nature—provided Griffiths with the "true answer" to the questions he faced about God and the world.

This little-known backstory helps to explain why Lewis sought to connect Barfield and Griffiths. All three were admirers of Coleridge's philosophical theology, but Lewis was the bridge between them. During a visit to Oxford in June 1930, Lewis told Griffiths of Barfield's desire to edit Coleridge's unpublished works. Griffiths, it seems, had only just "recently been turned inside out by Coleridge" and was eager to pursue the plan.[79] Lewis also shared that the project depended on financial support and the uncertain prospect of backing by the endowment of an American university. Lewis wrote to Barfield, though he worried that his meddling might occasion a rift in their friendship.

---

[77]Griffiths, *Golden String*, 49.
[78]Griffiths, *Golden String*, 49.
[79]*CLCSL* 3.1518 (June 18, 1930).

Figure 2.11. Owen Barfield

Whatever bashfulness Lewis claimed in relating these events to Barfield, he wrote freely a few days later to his longtime correspondent Arthur Greeves of the same situation, describing Griffiths with forthright admiration.[80] According to Lewis, Griffiths and two other friends—Hugh Waterman and Martyn Skinner—were now living almost entirely off the land and were willing to share their own annual income with Barfield in order to make the new Coleridge edition a reality if he were unable to find adequate financial support elsewhere. The three men were living in a commune at Cloud Farm (west of Porlock, in Somerset), supported by £800 annually, an egregious amount that might in part be devoted to better causes. With Lewis's help, they thereby proposed that Barfield accept £100 a year in support of the project.

During these pivotal years, Lewis, Barfield, and Griffiths each discovered in Coleridge's Anglican theology a new outlook on faith in the modern world, though each pursued very different spiritualities later. Barfield embraced anthroposophy, reinterpreting Coleridge in several studies including *What Coleridge Thought* (1971). Griffiths, for his part, took vows as a Benedictine monk and joined the Christian ashram movement in South India, where he became a yogi and spoke internationally as Swami Dayananda.[81]

---

[80]*CLCSL* 1.908 (June 22, 1930).

[81]For more information on Griffith's life, thought, and writings, see www.bedegriffiths .com/.

Lewis, as we all know, soon emerged as one of the foremost apologists for "mere" Christianity in the twentieth century.

A single notation at the back of Lewis's copy of Coleridge's *The Friend* may provide one long-overlooked aspect of his conversion to theism. The marginal comment, "First read. Jan 5th 1929,"[82] turns out to have come just as Lewis found his spiritual journey nearing its climax. The following year, Lewis's turn to theism would be

Figure 2.12. Bede Griffiths

complete, but that conversion did not come in a moment. Indeed, this same time marks the period that Griffiths identifies as the real commencement of their friendship. A short time after, Lewis finally "gave in, and admitted that God was God . . . the most dejected and reluctant convert in all England."[83] But he did not travel this road alone: his friends accompanied him, and they too were reading the English Romantic poet and philosopher Coleridge. Upon learning this little-known history, no one should be surprised that, years

Figure 2.13. Bede Griffiths

---

[82]C. S. Lewis marginalia in Coleridge, *The Friend*, 384. For other correspondence between Griffiths and Lewis around this time, see *CLCSL* 1.834, 858.

[83]Lewis, *Surprised by Joy*, 228-29.

later, Lewis dedicated his own conversion narrative, *Surprised by Joy*, to none other than Dom Bede Griffiths.

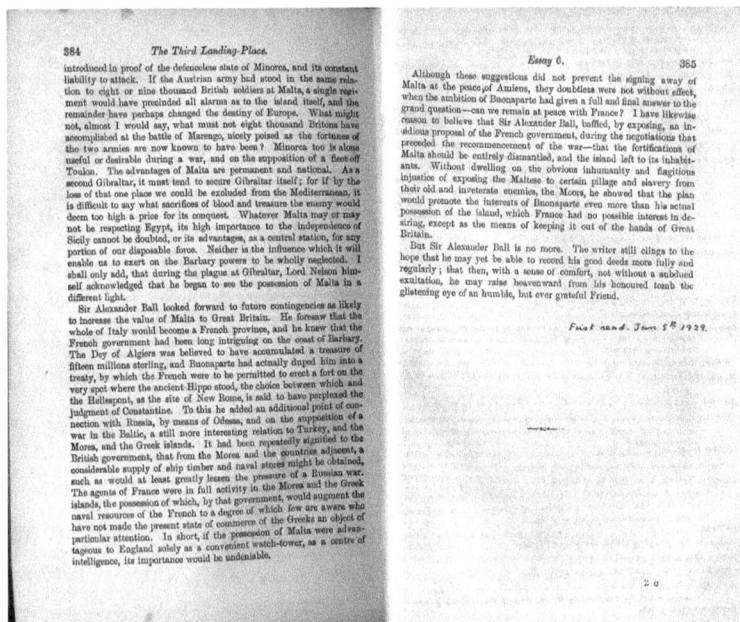

Figure 2.14. Marginal inscription by C. S. Lewis in Coleridge, *The Friend*, 384-85

INTERIOR LIFE

The influence of British Romanticism runs deep in the writings of C. S. Lewis. His memoir is best understood as a conversion narrative in the psychological vein of Romantic-era life writing, while his beloved examination of grief takes up life writing techniques in the evangelical tradition. In these works, we find Lewis drawing on two of the most influential English Romantics: William Wordsworth and Samuel Taylor Coleridge.

Lewis clearly worried that the Romantic emphasis on feeling and interiority might be abused. He both reflects and runs against the grain of his sources, embracing the religion of the heart even as he cautions readers against the potential for enthusiasm. How does a writer share lessons from personal life without risking the formation of a "suffocatingly subjective" narrative?

Let's return to the *Journal of Sarah Eliza Congdon*, who wrote in the heat of mid-nineteenth-century American Romantic revivalism. Congdon knew well the matters of Methodist heart religion, and her writing reflects the vicissitudes of lived experience. She dreams of her dead mother, meditates on trials and temptations, and worries that she will be damned. But, all the while, there is a sense of location—of concrete memory and a sense of place—that gives her journal an emotional immediacy that Lewis's memoirs of conversion and grief sometimes lack.

Surprised by Joy is characterized by its selectivity. This is not an account of sin that separates him from God. This is not Bunyan's *Grace Abounding to the Chief of Sinners*, with stories of cursing and game-playing on the Sabbath. Instead, Lewis's work is much closer to Scott's *Force of Truth* in its psychological depth—the sense that Lewis is working through the problem of atheism intellectually, just as Scott considered Unitarianism as a matter for rational deliberation. Yet Wordsworth's impact is also felt. Not only in the tantalizing title but also in the thousand ways that Lewis alludes to Romanticism, *Surprised by Joy* shows itself to be very much in the same spirit as Wordsworth's *Prelude*, for *Surprised by Joy* is the story of the growth of the would-be poet's mind, even as it is an account of his conversion.

Similarly, *A Grief Observed* maintains all the appearances of a journal of a troubled soul. He grieves the loss of his beloved, etching his pain into the page. But unlike the journal of Sarah Eliza Congdon, Lewis's work lacks the narrative uncertainty of a real, unfinished journal. The reader of Lewis's account knows that doubt will not win in the end. In this, *A Grief Observed* is more like John Wesley's *Journal*: while much remains in the life ahead, this is a composition ready for public consumption.

In Romantic studies, there is a much-discussed thesis about the sort of "anxiety of influence" that marks the great poets—ever aware of their intentional misreading of those who went before them. Lewis engages in just such an act in his own life writing, taking up his forebears and rereading the tradition for his own purposes. Nevertheless, at crucial points he remains less in command of the story than we might think. His narratives display what I call an "anxiety of memory," in which he reimagines the events of his own life according to the apologetic he seeks to advance. All authors do this, of course, only with Lewis the disquiet reveals itself in his uncertainty about precisely the Romantic interiority that he willingly embraces.

Of course, one might say that all writing is autobiographical in some sense. My own interest in Romanticism, Methodism, and what we call interiority shapes my thinking about Lewis. Indeed, how can I even tell readers about the remarkable journal of Sarah Eliza Congdon without noting that I, too, was born in Rhinebeck, New York—some 150 years after her—and that my early years were shaped by experiences of revivalism not entirely unlike her own. So, too, like many other readers of Lewis, I found in him both a kindred spirit in the converted life and a helpful antidote to the excesses of enthusiasm as I sought a stable, rational (even imaginative) ground on which to base my faith. The historical and the personal meet again and again.

In my final chapter, I will show how Lewis faced the problem of individual experience and sought out a solution in dialogue with the same Romantics who had accompanied him thus far on his journey. Through Romantic conceptions of the imagination, Lewis discovered a language that could mediate between heaven and earth. But this meant, for all his talk of longing for a glory that lay beyond, he found himself looking to what had always been immediately within his grasp.

RESPONSE
Matthew Lundin

One of the unexpected delights of reading Jeffrey Barbeau's chapter is learning about Sarah Congdon. As a historian, I found my heart "strangely warmed" by her diary and by Barbeau's story of discovering it in the Wheaton College archives. In its irreducible particularity, the diary challenges the reader to imagine the world of revival-swept western New York and a young schoolteacher's place within it. In passages recording her spiritual anxieties and doubts, we catch brief glimpses of a young woman turning to a popular spiritual genre to wrestle with questions about her identity, her relationships, her place in the world, and her eternal destiny. Like so many historical sources, the diary invites us to read between the lines. What unspoken social, economic, and personal concerns might Congdon have been translating into a religious idiom? To ask such questions is not to engage in a cynical project of "seeing through" the source. Rather, it is to acknowledge the complexity of human subjectivity—and the incarnational truth that God meets us in the midst of our particular, embodied contexts, with all their uncertainty and unresolved tension.

For these reasons, many of us would be reluctant to call Congdon's diary "suffocatingly subjective." And yet this was precisely what Lewis worried readers might think of his own spiritual autobiography. As Barbeau explains, Lewis's word of warning was a rhetorical move, a signal that something more was at stake than mere personal disclosure. For Lewis, autobiographical writing was part of an apologetic project. Thanks to Barbeau's brilliant research into Lewis's notes and marginalia, we now know just how Romantic that project was. Lewis aimed to show that readers could find within themselves a universal yearning ("joy") that provided proof of God. Paradoxically, subjective experience offered an escape from subjectivism. Within the self was "a road right out of the self" to something "sheerly objective."[1] For Lewis, the goal of autobiographical writing was to show, through a process of elimination, that subjective experience revealed a transcendent desire that was universal, irreducible, and incapable of being satisfied with anything other than God.

In appealing to inner feeling, Lewis had many examples to follow, and Barbeau shows how familiar Lewis was with both Methodist and Romantic models of life writing. Yet the influence of these models was rarely direct, and Lewis's ambivalence about emotion and subjectivity—his "anxiety of memory"—was perhaps even more pronounced than Barbeau suggests. Romantic and Methodist life writing emerged when appeals to natural sentiment and religious feeling enjoyed broad cultural appeal and intellectual legitimacy.[2] Lewis, by contrast, wrote in an age skeptical of such appeals. He was aware that arguments from experience or feeling left him vulnerable to charges of the very subjectivism he sought to escape. Thus, even as he turned to human psychology and personal experience to establish evidence for God, Lewis warned readers against any attempt to emotionalize, psychologize, or "see through" his experience.[3] For Lewis, there was a real risk of producing a "suffocatingly subjective" work—a risk he resisted at every turn, seeking to cordon off theological and metaphysical truths from the contingencies of personal experience.

This resistance can be seen in the strikingly unemotional way Lewis narrates his spiritual experiences. Although *Surprised by Joy*

---

[1] C. S. Lewis, *Surprised by Joy: The Shape of My Early Life* (Boston: Mariner, 2012), 221.
[2] For a historical explanation of the emotional regime of "sentimentality," see William M. Reddy, *The Navigation of Feeling: A Framework for the History of Emotions* (New York: Cambridge University Press, 2001).
[3] C. S. Lewis, *The Abolition of Man, or Reflections on Education with Special Reference to the Teaching of English in the Upper Forms of Schools* (New York: Macmillan, 1947), 50.

and *A Grief Observed* begin with unabashed expressions of feeling—yearning and grief—they culminate with spiritual encounters that are the opposite of Methodist enthusiasm. Instead of John Wesley's heart "strangely warmed," we learn of a weighty choice that was "strangely unemotional." As Lewis remembers it, "I was moved by no desires or fears."[4] Similarly, in recounting how a brush with death during World War I gave him a glimpse of the transcendent self behind consciousness, Lewis describes a moment of pure intellectual perception: "as unemotional as something in a textbook."[5] In his meditations on grief, the narrator presents his spiritual encounter with his deceased spouse not as a "rapturous re-union" but rather as a "business-like" presence.[6] Here we see Lewis keen to portray spiritual encounters as objective experiences, beyond any suspicion of "enthusiasm." There is something decidedly Kantian about Lewis's descriptions of his experiences; they attempt to place religious feeling outside the realm of phenomenal perception altogether.

In the same way, Lewis's autobiographical texts self-consciously resist material explanations. They are full of warnings not to reduce his experiences to sex or class or to infer too much from what he omits.[7] The central argument of *Surprised by Joy* is that there is a longing in humans that cannot be contextualized, that cannot be explained away. But defending "immortal longings" against materialism was a more difficult task for a twentieth-century autobiographer than for a nineteenth-century Romantic poet.[8] Writing after

---

[4]Given Lewis's familiarity with Wesley and Methodism, it is likely the parallel language here was no accident (Lewis, *Surprised by Joy*, 224).

[5]Lewis, *Surprised by Joy*, 197.

[6]C. S. Lewis, *A Grief Observed* (Greenwich, CT: Seabury, 1963), 57-58.

[7]Lewis, *Surprised by Joy*, 30. One might note here that Lewis provided potential ammunition for Freudian interpretations by telling us that such a tendency for inference was a vice of his father.

[8]In the preface to the third edition of *Pilgrim's Regress*, Lewis characterized the major philosophical trends of the interwar era as sharing an animosity for "immortal longings"

Feuerbach, Darwin, Freud, and Marx, Lewis was aware that earlier Romantic appeals to emotion and intuition could be explained as products of psychology, evolutionary biology, or social conditioning. Thus, he sought to anticipate the arguments of potential critics. In the words of the narrator of *A Grief Observed*, "If this was a throw-up from my unconscious, then my unconscious must be a far more interesting region than the depth psychologists have led me to expect."[9] For Lewis, autobiographical writing risked furnishing contemporary readers with evidence for psychologizing—and thereby dismissing— the very "immortal longings" he turned to autobiography to prove.

These conundrums, I think, help to explain why Lewis's self-writing lacks the immediacy of Sarah Congdon's journal. In *Surprised by Joy*, personal contingencies are valuable less for their own sake than for the proof they offer of "joy," an innate desire that in solitude—or what the Romantics might have called "retirement"— seeks something independent of any biological, social, or psychological need.[10] Here, experience has a negative or corrective function. It is through repeated frustration and a process of elimination that the self comes to realize that its yearning cannot be satisfied with any finite thing.[11] This method of abstracting from context stands at the center not only of Lewis's autobiographical works but also of some of his most famous apologetic arguments. It lies behind Lewis's majestic—and majestically Romantic—image in *The Weight of Glory* of the individual as an immortal, infinitely greater than cultures and civilizations.[12]

When taken to an extreme, this Romantic apologetic risked devaluing the material world and abstracting the self entirely from its

(C. S. Lewis, *The Pilgrim's Regress: An Allegorical Apology for Christianity, Reason and Romanticism* [London: Geoffrey Bles, 1943], 10).

[9]Lewis, *Grief Observed*, 58.

[10]Lewis, *Surprised by Joy*, 221.

[11]Lewis, *Pilgrim's Regress*, 10.

[12]C. S. Lewis, *The Weight of Glory and Other Addresses* (New York: Macmillan, 1949), 15.

embodied contexts. But here again, Lewis resisted the full pull of Romantic subjectivity, especially in its more grandiose forms. The landscape of nineteenth-century Romanticism was expansive; the self found itself reflected in vistas, outlooks, mountains, forests, lakes, and oceans. The most famous example of such a landscape is Caspar David Friedrich's painting *Wanderer Above the Sea of Fog*, which shows a bourgeois subject high on a peak, surveying a sublime panorama of cloud-shrouded mountains and treetops below.[13] By the early twentieth century, this expansive Romantic subjectivity had devolved, at least in some quarters, into an aggressive and narcissistic irrationalism, a celebration of the power of will to remake the world in its image.

Take, for instance, Nazi propagandist Joseph Goebbels, who was born just a year earlier than Lewis. In the early 1920s, before he had joined the Nazi Party, Goebbels completed a dissertation on nineteenth-century German Romanticism and struggled to find publishers for his sentimental nature poetry and expressionist plays. As a lapsed Catholic and unemployed author, Goebbels attempted to resolve his alienation and doubt through sheer will, scribbling in his diary, "It doesn't matter what we believe so long as we believe," "the greater and stronger I make

Figure 2.15. Caspar David Friedrich, *Wanderer Above the Sea of Fog* (ca. 1817)

---

[13]"More programmatically than perhaps any other painting of the period," Friedrich's painting "aspires to invoke the sublime of a thoroughly subjectivized aesthetic, in which the painted world turns inward on the beholder" (Joseph Leo Koerner, *Caspar David Friedrich and the Subject of Landscape* [New Haven, CT: Yale University Press, 1990], 181).

God, the greater and stronger I am myself," and "I believe, therefore I am."[14] This was the Romantic subject's quest for the absolute gone haywire.

Such unbounded and unhinged self-assertion is quite alien to Lewis's autobiographical writing. For all the grandeur of his vision of human destiny, the sphere of action in Lewis's narratives is mundane, ordinary, hemmed in. *Surprised by Joy* is full of small spaces, restricted vistas and views—homes, gardens, train stations, chess games, books. None of this should surprise us from an author who imagined a wardrobe as a portal. In the end, Lewis does not approach God; God approaches him. The famous conversion scene in *Surprised by Joy* occurs in his study. Hunched over his books, Lewis senses the "unrelenting approach" of the one "I so earnestly desired not to meet."[15] In Lewis's narrative, the Romantic pursuit of "joy"—often frustrated, often misdirected—can only go so far. It remains merely a preparation for divine grace.

---

[14]Joseph Goebbels, *Die Tagebücher von Joseph Goebbels: sämtliche Fragmente*, ed. Elke Fröhlich (Munich: K. G. Saur, 2004), 1/1:40, 89.

[15]Lewis, *Surprised by Joy*, 228.

Three

C. S. LEWIS AND THE
SACRAMENTAL IMAGINATION

Symbol Making

Late 1800s. The details will always remain a bit uncertain. Nevertheless, it's not hard to imagine the natural origin of a symbol now known around the world.

Envision a grassy space enveloped in shrubs and dense peat. The ground cover is squishy and wet. In places, a walker could sink down, perhaps as far as one's knees. Beneath the heavy peat, a fallen tree that once stood along the edge of the soggy bog lies undisturbed. For hundreds and perhaps thousands of years, the old oak has rested in this damp place, unaffected by the ordinary process of organic decomposition. Lacking access to oxygen in this low-nutrient, high-humidity tomb, the tumbled oak hardens as a sub-fossil wood that is characteristically dense with deep, dark coloration from tannins in the water.[1]

---

[1]C. Meneghello et al., "Bog Oak: Characteristics and Characterization of a Log from the Venetian Plain (Italy)," *Journal of Archaeological Science: Reports* 43 (2022): 103473; Irish Peatland Conservation Council, "Information Sheets: Bog Wood" (1996), https://web .archive.org/web/20071118224335/http://www.ipcc.ie/infobogwood.html.

In the eighteenth and nineteenth centuries, carpenters valued bog oak (also called "black oak" or "Irish oak") as a popular source for homebuilding, tools, and furniture in Ireland and parts of northern and central Europe. The natural wood requires no additional staining for use in trade goods. Once dry, a craftsman can trust that its hardness will last generations, resistant to pests and able to withstand the rigors of use over long periods of time. In nineteenth-century Ireland, there was no better choice than bog oak for a craftsman who wished to create a piece of furniture that could last for generations.

The exact origin of the wood in question will always remain something of a mystery, but the artisan who prepared this piece of furniture is not: Richard Lewis II, the paternal grandfather of C. S. Lewis. Hand-carved with an intricate front panel, the wardrobe sitting in the museum of the Marion E. Wade Center stands nearly seven feet tall, four feet wide, and two-and-a-half feet deep. According to the Lewis Family Papers, Richard Lewis was a boilermaker with the Cork Steamship Company, "yard manager at Dublin, and partner in a ship building firm at Belfast."[2] Richard Lewis first adzed the wood with a sharp, curved blade, then constructed

Figure 3.1. Lewis family wardrobe

---

[2]W. H. (Warren Hamilton) Lewis, ed., *Memoirs of the Lewis Family, 1850–1930*, vol. 1 (Oxford Leeborough, 1933), family tree, facing p. 233; my thanks to Laura Stanifer for her assistance.

the wardrobe from the various boards, before carving the panels in a series of intricate floral designs.

I have paid many visits to Lewis's wardrobe over the years, but one day I took time to sit before it in meditative study. The longer I spent with the wardrobe, the more I began to see and appreciate the skilled craftwork in its design. Boards of different shapes and sizes frame the top and sides, with beveled edges and curved surfaces that are smooth to my skin as I press my hand firmly along its lines. At the bottom, its four feet are each carefully etched with leaf-like patterns that distinguish the base with depth and sturdiness matched with expanding delicacy. It's the intricate design-work of the front, however, that immediately catches a visitor's eye: twenty-six inset floral carvings run vertical along each side, and more than fifty other blooms of varying shapes and sizes frame the remainder of the front panels. Metalwork, Richard Lewis's specialty, is also visible in the hand-wrought nails, locks, and hinges that hold the old boards together. These subtle features, pressed flush against the wood, match the dark grain of the old oak surface.

Stories about this legendary wardrobe abound. C. S. Lewis's cousin recalled that, as children, they would play in the wardrobe together in Lewis's family home in Little Lea, Belfast. Huddled together, young Jack would delight his brother and their cousins with "tales of adventure" in the close confines of these panels.[3]

But as I sit before the wardrobe in a brief interlude of quiet, I find myself suddenly alert to its deeper significance. For while the materiality of the wardrobe is fascinating—indeed, ecologists could examine the same wood for scientific study of an ancient place and time—the significance of this unique wardrobe relates directly to the stories that have been told about its literary doppelganger. For, as any reader of the Chronicles of Narnia knows, this is no ordinary wardrobe.

---

[3] Unpublished letter from Claire Clapperton to Clyde S. Kilby, August 20, 1979 (Wade).

I'm sitting on the floor gazing up at the carved panels when a small group of guests arrive in the museum. I scoot out of the way for this threesome. They barely notice me, but I know where they are headed. I have decided to watch silently as the scene plays out before my eyes. Prior to the pandemic, when numbers dropped precipitously, some ten thousand people came to the Marion E. Wade Center each year. Numbers are beginning to build again, and with every visitor comes an almost instinctual, reverential liturgy of ritual observance.

"This is so cool," the young woman whispers as she stands before the wardrobe. Her arms reach down passively, until carefully, almost fearfully, she pries a single panel door a few inches open. She is frozen, refusing to expose the interior fully, watching anxiously as if to see what might happen next. Her friends stand at a distance, taking photos of the moment, providing a record of the encounter to remember and share with others. She finally steps closer, exposing the interior to view. The woman now stands before the coats on display within, pressing them cautiously to the side to see what lies beyond. "So cool," she whispers again, almost inaudibly.

What makes this wardrobe such a meaningful symbol? And what does it signify to the one who makes a pilgrimage to stand before it? These are questions I hope to shed light on in this third and final chapter, for the answers take us back to the heart of British Romanticism and the legacy C. S. Lewis conveyed in his writings.

In the preceding chapters, I traced the influence of modern theology and Romantic literature on C. S. Lewis in an exploration of feeling, experience, and subjectivity. In the first chapter, I showed how Lewis's reading in modern theology and philosophy—the German heritage of Schleiermacher, through Hegel, and rising to its most skeptical conclusions in Feuerbach—shaped his approach to Christian apologetics in works such as *Mere Christianity*. Then I explained how the British Romantic poets gave voice to feeling and imagination in poetry that contributed to Lewis's own sense of identity as a budding poet and advocate for the moral life in *The Abolition of Man.*

In the second chapter, I focused on Lewis's writing about his own life—especially his two most popular memoirs, *Surprised by Joy* and *A Grief Observed*—and explained how literary practices of Methodist piety shaped British Romantic autobiography and, in turn, Lewis's personal compositions. In this, the legacy of Methodism, mediated by the poetics of William Wordsworth and the philosophical theology of Samuel Taylor Coleridge, contributed to Lewis's gradual (if seemingly sudden) conversion from atheism to theism and provided models for the sorts of autobiographical writing he used as apologetic instruments.

As these earlier chapters make clear, Lewis writes about individual experience far more than some of his interpreters have been willing to admit. In part, this is due to Lewis's own expressed anxieties: he measures his comments on the personal in rhetorical wordplay and cautions against an overdependence on individual experience in matters of faith. Yet this energetic display of tension between what might be called the interior and exterior is also a legacy of the Romantic Age. In one marginal comment in his copy of Herman Melville's *Moby Dick*, Lewis enigmatically asks whether the nineteenth-century greats hinted at challenges to be faced in the twentieth: "I wonder arc Melville, Emerson, Nietzche [*sic*], Carlyle & a few other in Nineteenth Century rumblings of the great collapse wh. came in our own?"[4] In Rosalind Murray's *The Life of Faith* (1943), a single marginal line—the only one in the book—offers a tantalizing clue to Lewis's anxieties about faith in the modern age: "The modern world reacts against the whole conception of truth revealed from above as a degradation of the human

---

[4]Marginalia by C. S. Lewis in Herman Melville, *Moby Dick; or the White Whale*, Everyman's Library (London: J. M. Dent, 1928), reverse of front free endpaper (C. S. Lewis Library collection, Wade).

intellect; it does not object in the same way to revelation 'from below'; the convictions which surge up from our own subconscious, from the undeveloped self. These are given generous consideration; these must on no account be repressed."[5]

In this final chapter, I consider the legacy of the Romantic "symbol" as the key to understanding Lewis's effort to negotiate personal experience. Such a study requires that we take account of his thoughts on nature, imagination, and the numinous. In the end, this leads to a clearer understanding of the role that the church and its narratives might play in the process of spiritual formation and even requires a fresh assessment of Lewis's place in the Christian tradition.

Nature's Beauty

Let's return to the "hard-bitten officer" described at the start of the fourth part of *Mere Christianity*. Interrupted during a lecture on theology, Lewis admits what we might be surprised to discover: the man had likely had a true encounter with God out in the desert, alone in the night. His experience was real, Lewis says. He had no reason to doubt it. Indeed, Lewis even confesses what some might wish to deny: the creeds of the church and even the stories recorded in the Bible are "less real" and "less exciting" than the "tremendous mystery" the officer confronted in that moment.

The admission comes with a warning, nevertheless. While personal experiences of the numinous may be real, they remain woefully limited. This seems to have influenced Lewis's own life writing, if his cautionary statements against the "suffocatingly subjective" in the preface to *Surprised by Joy* are any measure. For just these reasons, Lewis obliquely advises against the construction of a religion based on "feeling God in nature, and so on" in *Mere Christianity*.[6]

---

[5]Marginalia in Rosaline Murray, *The Life of Faith* (London: Centenary, 1943), 26 (C. S. Lewis Library collection, Wade).

[6]C. S. Lewis, *Mere Christianity* (New York: HarperOne, 2000), 155.

Lewis may have had one of his favorite poets in mind. In "Lines Composed a Few Miles Above Tintern Abbey," Wordsworth says of nature just what many feared of the early Romantic movement:

> That on the banks of this delightful stream
> We stood together; and that I, so long
> A worshipper of Nature, hither came
> Unwearied in that service[7]

The association between God and nature is something of a commonplace in early British Romanticism, but Wordsworth is among the most striking representatives of this theme. In *The Prelude*, Wordsworth repeatedly intimates divinity in the encounter with nature, as in his ascent of Mount Snowdon, in Wales, which I recalled in the first chapter:

> A meditation rose in me that night
> Upon the lonely Mountain when the scene
> Had passed away, and it appeared to me
> The perfect image of a mighty Mind,
> Of one that feeds upon infinity,
> That is exalted by an underpresence,
> The sense of God, or whatso'er is dim
> Or vast in its own being . . .[8]

Nevertheless, the key to such experiences of nature is not strictly the landscape. Rather, for Wordsworth, the landscape presents opportunities for individual growth when recollected afterwards in reflection. Such "spots of time" prove essential to our formation, as moments when

---

[7]Wordsworth, "Lines Written a Few Miles Above Tintern Abbey," lines 151-54, in *Wordsworth's Poetry and Prose*, Norton critical ed., ed. Nicholas Halmi (New York: Norton, 2014), 70.

[8]William Wordsworth, *The Prelude* (1805), book 13.66-73, in *Wordsworth's Poetry and Prose*, 367.

Figure 3.2. J. J. Dodd, *Snowdon from Nantlle Lakes* (1854)

> . . . our minds
> Are nourished and invisibly repaired;
> A virtue by which pleasure is enhanced,
> That penetrates, enables us to mount
> When high, more high, and lifts us up when fallen.[9]

Thus, for Wordsworth, nature's power is discovered not only in an immediate sense of terror or peace but also in the tranquility of memory, when time has passed and the images of past events enliven us, sustain us, and prompt personal growth.

Coleridge, too, often writes of nature's ministerial power. In the conversation poem "Frost at Midnight," the narrator muses before the sleeping baby at his side, declaring allegiance to nature's capacity, "But *thou*, my babe! shalt wander like a breeze / By lakes and sandy

---

[9]Wordsworth, *Prelude*, book 11.264-68, in *Wordsworth's Poetry and Prose*, 353.

shores, beneath the crags / Of ancient mountain, and beneath the clouds."[10]

The encounter with nature makes possible an encounter with the divine:

> so shalt thou see and hear
> The lovely shapes and sounds intelligible
> Of that eternal language, which thy God
> Utters, who from eternity doth teach
> Himself in all, and all things in himself.[11]

The underlying philosophy for such claims derives, in part, from the influence of David Hartley. In brief, Hartley's *Observations on Man* (1749) proposes that all living things contain a vital energy that connects the human mind to the originating divine cause. The result is a materialistic philosophy of necessitarianism that connects all life. It also points to the prospect of pantheism, a religious philosophy that Coleridge identified chiefly with Spinoza.

Coleridge was so influenced by Hartley's work that he named his son—the baby sleeping silently by his side in "Frost at Midnight"—Hartley Coleridge. Yet Coleridge, in time, rejected Hartley's philosophy. Nature must remain subordinate to mind. As a result, the centrality of the landscape gradually recedes in importance in Coleridge's writings, opening the way for a broader conception of the relationship between nature and the self.

The Romantic legacy of nature worship is just what Lewis is reacting to in his comments on the subject in *The Four Loves* (1960). In the chapter "Likings and Loves for the Sub-Human," Lewis offers an extended discussion of nature, a form of impersonal love deserving of special treatment. Lewis has Wordsworth very much in mind—and tells readers why the love of nature so often goes wrong.

---

[10]Samuel Taylor Coleridge, "Frost at Midnight," in *Poetical Works*, 3 vols. in 6 parts, ed. J. C. C. Mays (Princeton, NJ: Princeton University Press, 2001), I.1.456.54-56.
[11]Coleridge, "Frost at Midnight," in *Poetical Works* I.1.456.58-62.

He begins by noting that the "love of nature" that he refers to is not merely a love for the beautiful. This is not about flowers, mountains, or animals. These, he thinks, are the sort of particulars that a botanist or even a landscape painter might attend to but with such a degree of interest that the lover of nature would inevitably be annoyed.[12]

Rather, the sort of individual that Lewis invokes is best represented by Wordsworth, "their spokesman." For Wordsworth, according to Lewis, it's not beauty that the lover of nature really wants. Rather, it's the spirit of the place, whether beautiful and harmonious or bleak and dreary: "They want to absorb it into themselves, to be coloured through and through by it."[13]

Lewis thinks that such a love of nature only goes just so far; others may look on a similar landscape and see not goodness and beauty but amoral competition. Nature calls out to such degeneracy, confirming only what our base instincts had already determined to be true. Nature does not teach but only validates the human desire for sex and power, endorsing and authenticating what we have already decided to see.[14]

So whether we "love" nature in what Lewis refers to as the "Wordsworthian" sense of rapture or in the darker vision of untamed power, he thinks it cannot produce a philosophy or theology. Instead, Lewis claims that nature only provides icons or images with which we might dress individual convictions. Nature provides an objective, exterior confirmation that *incarnates* beliefs that we either already know or have learned elsewhere. Thus, for example, nature

---

[12]Though I think Lewis would have appreciated the work of my predecessor in this lecture series, Kristen Page, *The Wonders of Creation: Learning Stewardship from Narnia and Middle-Earth*, Hansen Lectureship Series (Downers Grove, IL: IVP Academic, 2022).

[13]C. S. Lewis, *The Four Loves* (New York: HarperCollins, 1960), 23. Notably, Bede Griffiths articulates a similar concern at the beginning of his memoir, *The Golden String* (1954).

[14]Lewis, *Four Loves*, 24. Tantalizingly, Lewis identifies a passage on natural religion in his personal index in a copy of John Henry Newman's *Parochial and Plain Sermons* that discusses the limits of nature in matters of sin, conscience, and the cosmos (vol. 1 of 8 [London: Longmans, Green, 1919–1924], in C. S. Lewis Library collection, Wade).

cannot prove the existence of "a God of glory and of infinite majesty," but it can illustrate what such a glory may mean. Moreover, nature cannot attest to the "fear of God," but the experience of "certain ominous ravines and unapproachable crags" can move us to a depth of reverence for the divine beyond trifling platitudes about safety.[15]

All such qualifications may leave Lewis's readers feeling rather downcast about the potential for any love of nature whatsoever. No doubt, his tone is largely cautionary and certainly lacks the sort of numinous experience discovered while rambling through wild and rugged landscapes that Wordsworth and Coleridge made famous in their earliest poetic experiments. Yet there are also signs that Lewis knew that these poets began gradually to see nature from a new perspective, shifting from their early pantheism to a robust idealism that continued to revere nature's pedagogical capacity.

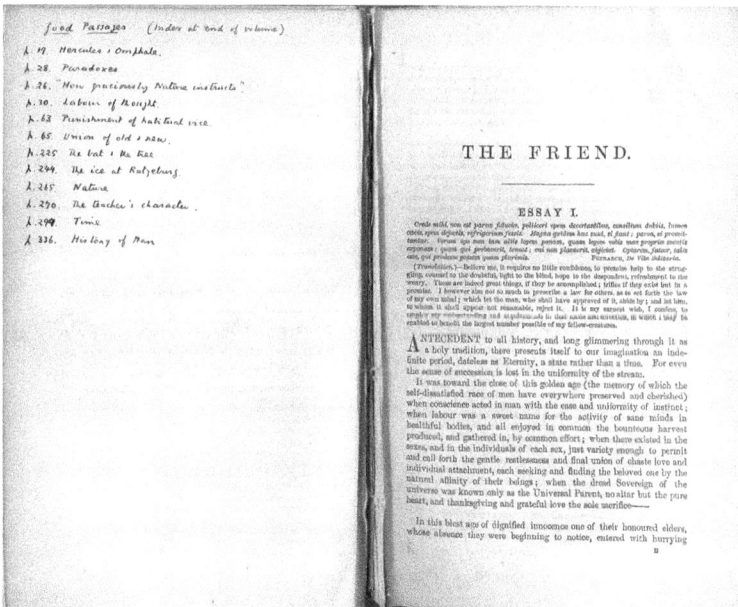

Figure 3.3. Marginalia by C. S. Lewis in Coleridge, *The Friend*

[15]Lewis, *Four Loves*, 26.

Unpublished marginalia in Lewis's personal copy of Coleridge's *The Friend* may provide fresh insight. Opposite the published table of contents near the front of this book—the same volume that he read as he came nearer and nearer to theism—Lewis records a series of "Good Passages" including an illustration on "Nature."[16] The selection stems from a letter *"To the Editor of the Friend,"* who objects to Coleridge's emphasis on nature and imagination in prior issues (the work originally appeared in serial format). Such writing leads only too quickly to "false pretensions," "self-delusion," and "enthusiasm kindling among multiplying images of greatness and beauty."[17]

Against the critic, Coleridge presents a lengthy response by none other than William Wordsworth. Lewis marginally lines several pages of the corresponding text, including an illuminating discussion of an otherwise ordinary experience: the child who observes as the light of a candle wanes in the darkness of night. As the extinguished flame fades, revives, and finally vanishes, the child watches, "bound to it by a spell."[18] Then when the same individual, years later, seeks to understand the decline and death of a beloved parent or friend, that image returns again: "A world of fresh sensation will gradually open upon him as his mind puts off its infirmities. . . . He makes it his prime business to understand himself. New sensations, I affirm, will be opened out—pure and sanctioned by that reason which is their original author . . . and, in this sense, he may be said to measure back the track of life he has trod."[19]

[16]Marginalia by C. S. Lewis, in Samuel Taylor Coleridge, *The Friend* (London: Bell & Daldy, 1865), verso of table of contents (C. S. Lewis Library collection, Wade).

[17]Coleridge, *The Friend* (1865), 251, 254; cf. Samuel Taylor Coleridge, *The Friend*, 2 vols., ed. Barbara E. Rooke (Princeton, NJ: Princeton University Press, 1969), 380, 383.

[18]Marginalia in Coleridge, *The Friend* (1865), 266; cf. *The Friend* (1969), 398.

[19]Marginalia in Coleridge, *The Friend* (1865), 267; cf. *The Friend* (1969), 399.

Another item on Lewis's list of "Good Passages" in *The Friend* is one labeled, "How graciously Nature instructs."[20] In the corresponding section, Coleridge explains, "[Nature] cannot give us the knowledge derived from sight without occasioning us at first to mistake images of reflection for substances."[21] The initial mistake proves helpful in the end, however, since "the very consequences of the delusion lead inevitably to its detection; and out of the ashes of the error rises a new flower of knowledge." In other words, Coleridge thinks that nature provides images that allow us to recognize truths we might otherwise neglect. To those who object to Nature *tout court*, those "hurrying enlighteners and revolutionary amputators" of Nature's gentle promptings, Coleridge refers to the manner in which "the dry foliage" of the oak or beech tree is cast off "by the propulsion of the new buds, that supply its place."[22] The viewer of nature may "mistake images of reflection for substances," but the consequence of the error will yield new insight into the truth of the matter with time. Indeed, some errors in perception are better than complete intellectual blindness: "My friends!" Coleridge concludes, "a clothing even of withered leaves is better than bareness."[23]

So while Lewis objects to the broadly Wordsworthian claim that nature "teaches" in *The Four Loves,* I suspect he's actually not far from Coleridge's exposition of nature and imagination in *The Friend.* In fact, the passage that most likely inspired the critical letter was one that Lewis also highlights in his list of "Good Passages": "The ice at Ratzeburg." There, Coleridge describes personal experiences of sublime beauty and terror at the Lake of Ratzeburg, Germany. In one, a "storm of wind" blasted the frozen lake all night

---

[20]Marginalia by C. S. Lewis in Coleridge, *The Friend* (1865), verso of table of contents (C. S. Lewis Library collection, Wade).

[21]Coleridge, *The Friend* (1865), 26; cf. *The Friend* (1969), 1:47-48.

[22]Coleridge, *The Friend* (1865), 26; cf. *The Friend* (1969), 1:47 48.

[23]Coleridge, *The Friend* (1865), 26; cf. *The Friend* (1969), 1:47-48.

through: "such were the thunders and howlings of the breaking ice, that they have left a conviction on my mind, that there are sounds more sublime than any sight can be, more absolutely suspending the power of comparison, and more utterly absorbing the mind's self-consciousness in its total attention to the object working upon it."[24] Immediately following, Coleridge includes a selection from Wordsworth's yet-unpublished *Prelude*, including his assertion that the soul is elevated

> with enduring things,
> With life and nature: purifying thus
> The elements of feeling and of thought,
> And sanctifying by such discipline [. . .]
> A grandeur in the beatings of the heart.[25]

As we will see, Coleridge, Wordsworth, and Lewis each embrace such striking language because they all maintained a theory of perception that distinguishes between the sensuous and supersensuous.

For his part, Lewis cautioned against nature worship even as he continued to affirm nature's power. Nature's beauty would not be lost to us if only we maintain the order of our loves. When the beauty of nature becomes the goal of the spiritual life, it quickly becomes a religion. If a religion, then nature is a god. If a god, then a demon above all. Alternately, if the love of nature provides a context for the love of God, then Lewis thinks nature may serve as a helpful, perhaps essential, framework for devotion: "Say your prayers in a garden early, ignoring steadfastly the dew, the birds, and the flowers, and you will come away overwhelmed by its freshness and joy; go there in order to be overwhelmed and, after a certain age, nine times out of ten nothing will happen to

---

[24]Coleridge, *The Friend* (1865), 244 (C. S. Lewis Library collection, Wade); cf. *The Friend* (1969), 1:367.

[25]Wordsworth, "Growth of Genius . . . ," in *The Friend* (1865), 244; cf. *The Friend* (1969), 1:367.

you."[26] If only we will ignore nature, we will find ourselves aroused to a deeper longing and understanding of God than we ever thought possible.

VISIONARY LANGUAGE

If the language of "give up this one thing and you'll receive it back in a better form" sounds familiar, it's because Lewis appeals to just such an idea repeatedly in his works. Among the most engaging examples of this pattern appears in *The Great Divorce*. While on a journey toward heaven, Lewis's protagonist observes case after case of individuals who must give up earthly loves to proceed in their journey to the mountains.

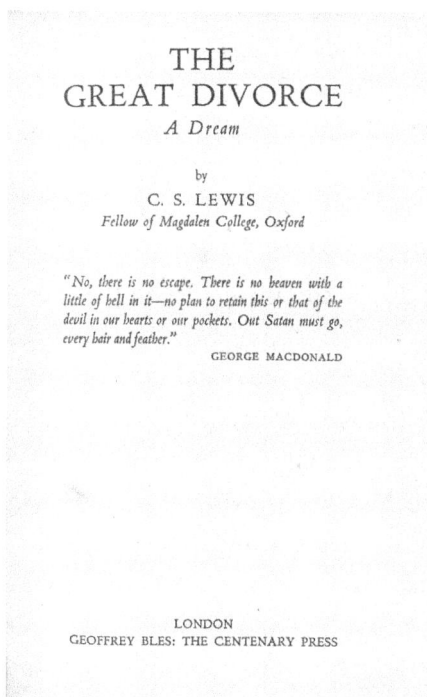

THE
GREAT DIVORCE
A Dream

by
C. S. LEWIS
Fellow of Magdalen College, Oxford

"*No, there is no escape. There is no heaven with a little of hell in it—no plan to retain this or that of the devil in our hearts or our pockets. Out Satan must go, every hair and feather.*"
GEORGE MACDONALD

LONDON
GEOFFREY BLES: THE CENTENARY PRESS

Figure 3.4. *The Great Divorce* (1945)

[26]Lewis, *Four Loves*, 28.

Consider the case of the artist. In that memorable scene of *The Great Divorce*, the artist and one of the solid "spirit" people discuss the beauty of the landscape around them. The artist would like to paint the scene, but the spirit responds by correcting him according to much the same logic applied two decades later in *The Four Loves*. Early in life, the painter had sought heaven in the signs and images he discerned on earth, but now the artist will need to learn to see properly, as if for the very first time.[27] The problem is not nature or beauty per se, then, but the way that love for creation may too easily replace love for the divine. Indeed, landscapes and embodied life figure prominently in the narrative, but the story of the artist reminds readers that all creation belongs to the category of "nature." Not only real trees and grasses, but also paintings, love shared among family or friends, and even the stories we tell amount to the stuff of "nature." Through any of these, we may find ourselves yearning after God or, alternately, come to prize earthly loves as ends in themselves.

Many readers will recall that *The Great Divorce* opens with prefatory remarks in which Lewis warns readers not to take his fantasy as theological speculation about the afterlife, but few will recall that the preface commences with a direct reference to British Romanticism. In the opening sentences, Lewis offers a seemingly innocuous explanation of his title and his indebtedness to William Blake's *Marriage of Heaven and Hell* (1790). "If I have written of their *Divorce*," Lewis explains, "this is not because I think myself a fit antagonist for so great a genius."[28] In Blake's illuminated book, etched in relief, the artist exemplifies his principle of contraries in a revolutionary prophecy fit for the times: "Without Contraries is no progression. Attraction and Repulsion, Reason and Energy, Love and Hate, are necessary to Human

---

[27]C. S. Lewis, *The Great Divorce: A Dream* (New York: HarperOne, 1973), 83.
[28]Lewis, *Great Divorce*, vii.

existence."[29] In Blake, though, the contraries are not a duality of opposites but principles in relationship.[30] Think of the "Little Lamb" and "Tyger, Tyger burning bright," respectively, in Blake's *Songs of Innocence* and *Songs of Experience*.

If *The Great Divorce* is in any sense a response to Blake's *Marriage of Heaven and Hell*, then the rejection of his theory of contraries is almost certainly in view. Lewis seems to say: we cannot have it both ways. Truth comes not in contraries but in the glimpse of heaven that earth provides. To embrace heaven, we must see earth for what it really is: a signpost along the road. Everywhere in *The Great Divorce* Lewis seems intent to remind his readers that "nature" is prompting us to press forward—amid trials and pains, no less—even if the real seems ever beyond the limits of our experience.[31]

Perhaps for this reason, Lewis concludes *The Great Divorce* with reference to another Romantic, bookending the entire work with two of the great poets of the movement. For just as Lewis begins with a recollection of William Blake, he ends with reference to Samuel Taylor Coleridge. In fact, the allusion is so oblique most readers may well not even see it, forgetting that *The Great Divorce* is subtitled *A Dream*. In fact, as the narrator observes a silver table with chessmen moved as puppets in the final chapter, the veil is pulled back on the entire journey. When the

---

[29]William Blake, *The Marriage of Heaven and Hell*, in *Blake's Poetry and Designs*, 2nd ed., Norton critical ed., ed. Mary Lynn Johnson and John E. Grant (New York: W. W. Norton, 2008), 69.

[30]For more on this, see Dan Miller, "Contrary Revelation: 'The Marriage of Heaven and Hell,'" *Studies in Romanticism* 24 (1985): 491-509.

[31]The increasing density of heaven in Lewis's *The Great Divorce* might be compared to John Wesley's eschatological vision in sermons such as "The New Creation" and "The General Deliverance," where all living things are restored and elevated—and even the animals, as in Narnia, are capable of speech: "They will be restored, not only to that measure of understanding which they had in paradise, but to a degree of it as much higher than that as the understanding of an elephant is beyond that of a worm" (John Wesley, "The General Deliverance," in *Sermons*, ed. Albert C. Outler [Nashville: Abingdon, 1984–1987], 2:446).

narrator wonders aloud whether all he had seen was merely a
fiction, all that he had heard only a deception, his guide responds,
"Do not ask of a vision in a dream more than a vision in a dream
can give."[32] Lewis's turn of phrase refers back to Coleridge's
famous poem "Kubla Khan," whose title is "Kubla Khan: Or, A
Vision in a Dream."

Much as the central figure in *The Great Divorce* abruptly wakes
to the sound of wartime sirens, the poet's recollection of a great
poem (written within a dream
state) in "Kubla Khan" is dis-
rupted by the notorious "person
from Porlock." The poem is
lost; only fragments remain.
The poet laments, longing for
that which he cannot fully describe or even remember:

Kubla Khan:

OR

A VISION IN A DREAM.

Figure 3.5. S. T. Coleridge, "Kubla Khan" (1816)

> Could I revive within me
> Her symphony and song,
> To such a deep delight 'twould win me,
> That with music loud and long,
> I would build that dome in air,
> That sunny dome! those caves of ice!
> And all who heard should see them there,
> And all should cry, Beware! Beware!
> His flashing eyes, his floating hair!
> Weave a circle round him thrice,
> And close your eyes with holy dread:
> For he on honey-dew hath fed,
> And drunk the milk of Paradise.[33]

[32]Lewis, *Great Divorce*, 143-44.
[33]Coleridge, "Kubla Khan," in *Poetical Works* I.1.514.

If this reference to Coleridge appears far-fetched, remember that Lewis identifies the first lines of "Kubla Khan" as precisely the sort of Romantic vision he was aiming for in denominating *A Pilgrim's Regress* nothing short of *An Allegorical Apology for Christianity, Reason and Romanticism*.[34]

MEASURELESS CAVERNS

Lewis's identification with the dream state at the close of *The Great Divorce* provides yet another reminder of his indebtedness to the Romantic imagination. Signs of Lewis's thinking along these lines are apparent everywhere in his writings. The marginalia, too, corroborate just such an inspiration.

A single marginal line in Lewis's personal copy of William Hazlitt's *Winterslow* provides an evocative hint. Hazlitt records his travel to the West Country and Wordsworth's Alfoxden House. He listens to Coleridge talk and Wordsworth reading from his latest poems, noting "In the outset of life (and particularly at this time I felt it so) our imagination has a body to it. We are in a state between sleeping and waking, and have indistinct but glorious glimpses of strange shapes, and there is always something to come better than what we see. As in our dreams the fulness of the blood."[35]

The association between dream states and imagination abounds in Romantic literature, as Lewis knew well. In John Keats's "Ode to Psyche," the poet describes the poetic task in the language of the dream state:

> O Goddess! hear these tuneless numbers, wrung
> By sweet enforcement and remembrance dear,
> And pardon that thy secrets should be sung

---

[34]C. S. Lewis, *The Pilgrim's Regress: An Allegorical Apology for Christianity, Reason and Romanticism*, illustrated by Michael Hague (Grand Rapids, MI: Eerdmans, 1992), 204.
[35]Marginalia in William Hazlitt, *Winterslow: Essays and Characters Written There* (London: H. Froude, 1906), 15 (C. S. Lewis Library collection, Wade).

Even into thine own soft-conchèd ear:
Surely I dreamt today, or did I see
The winged Psyche with awakened eyes?[36]

Figure 3.6. John Keats, by William Hilton (ca. 1822)

Similarly, the final couplet of Keats's "Ode to a Nightingale" appeals to reverie: "Was it a vision, or a waking dream? / Fled is that music:—Do I wake or sleep?"[37] The imagination of the poet is like a dream—partial or fragmentary—and suggestive of something known almost intuitively by the individual self. Lewis embraced just such a Romantic meaning in giving *The Great Divorce* the subtitle "*A Dream.*" In its origination within the embodied person, imagination remains at one with nature. Drops of laudanum, a knock at the door, or blaring sirens that warn of trouble overhead can each contribute to or diminish the creative act: "The imagination can act as an organ of the body and, in concert with translationary processes, become a physical part of dreams."[38] This is the same power that allows the individual to recognize menace in the looming mountain and the sublime beauty of the waterfall, but poetic imagination transforms the perception of a landscape in willed acts that "idealize and unify."[39]

---

[36]John Keats, "Ode to Psyche," in *Major British Writers*, enlarged ed., ed. G. B. Harrison (New York: Harcourt, Brace, 1959), 2.342.

[37]John Keats, "Ode to a Nightingale," in Harrison, *Major British Writers*, 2.344.

[38]Jennifer Ford, *Coleridge on Dreaming: Romanticism, Dreams and the Medical Imagination* (Cambridge: Cambridge University Press, 1998), 196.

[39]Samuel Taylor Coleridge, *Biographia Literaria*, ed. James Engell and W. Jackson Bate (Princeton, NJ: Princeton University Press, 1983), 1.304.

In this tradition, the artist combines sensory data and truth. Hazlitt's *Lectures on English Poets* refers to the manner in which imagination "represents objects not as they are in themselves, but as they are moulded by other thoughts and feelings." Lewis underlined the passage in his personal copy, summarizing the concept: "Poetry expresses what appears to the imagination: i.e. objects modified in a particular way."[40]

Thus Sara Coleridge, the daughter of Samuel Taylor Coleridge, describes her fairy tale *Phantasmion* as "a tissue of unrealities" that reflect "unity of conception and feeling throughout."[41] The work—often regarded as the first fantasy novel in the English language, and likely an inspiration for George MacDonald's *Phantastes*—was one that Lewis almost certainly knew of and may well have read.[42] Here, too, the dream state looms large, for Sara Coleridge includes more than forty references to dreams and dream states in *Phantasmion*. Characters experience positive and negative emotions, travel, and perceive the future during dreams. In her personal marginalia, she even describes how the landscape of her Lake District childhood provided the inspiration for much of the setting of her story of a prince, a princess, and the obstacles they face: "The Tale was . . . a dimly bright vista of fancy & dream invention. Doubtless the scenery of this

---

[40]Marginalia in William Hazlitt, *Lectures on English Poets and The Spirit of the Age* (London: J. M. Dent, 1910), 4 (C. S. Lewis Library collection, Wade).

[41]Sara Coleridge, *The Regions of Sara Coleridge's Thought: Selected Literary Criticism*, ed. Peter Swaab (New York: Palgrave Macmillan, 2012), 9; cf. Jeffrey W. Barbeau, *Sara Coleridge: Her Life and Thought* (New York: Palgrave Macmillan, 2014), 59-70.

[42]In Oliver Elton's *A Survey of English Literature,* for example, marginal lining and underlining appear in a passage devoted to Sara Coleridge's literary contribution: "The best writing of Sara Coleridge is found in her letters, though in the little fairy tale, *Phantasmion* (1837), there is a rich and fanciful inventiveness, and a feeling for colour unreal and magical, that beseems the daughter of Coleridge" (Oliver Elton, *A Survey of English Literature, 1780–1830* [London: E. Arnold, 1924], 133; C. S. Lewis Library collection, Wade). Excerpts from Sara Coleridge's writing on her father also appear in D. G. James's *The Romantic Comedy* (London: Oxford University Press, 1948), 226-27, a work that Lewis heavily annotated (C. S. Lewis Library collection, Wade).

passage was my native Lake by moon-light transported into fairy-land and faërized."[43]

The Romantic link to Lewis proves illuminating in any analysis of mind, nature, and dream states in his writings. In fact, in his index to Coleridge's *The Friend*, Lewis singles out dream states as a point of particular emphasis: "DREAMS, awakening from p. 37—oscillations between sleep and wakening the true 'witching time' p. 85—hints for, furnished by outward objects. p. 89."[44]

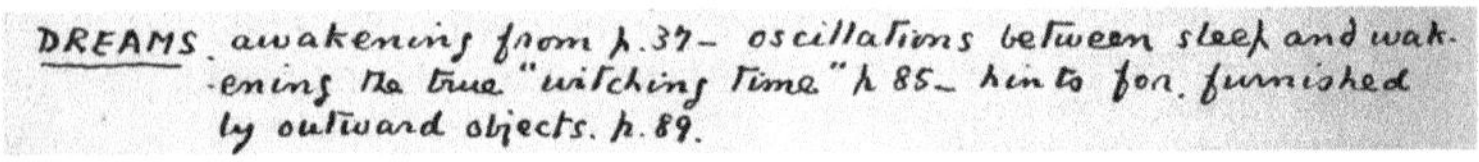
DREAMS. awakening from p. 37— oscillations between sleep and wak-ening the true "witching time" p. 85— hints for. furnished by outward objects. p. 89.

Figure 3.7. Marginalia by C. S. Lewis in Coleridge, *The Friend*

For Coleridge, the dream state reflects not only inward dispositions but the memory of past events: "I have long wished to devote an entire work to the subject of dreams, visions, ghosts, witchcraft . . . either from books or from personal testimony."[45] Why? Because Coleridge thought the dream state revealed the connection between parts and the whole: "the great law of the imagination," in which "a likeness in part tends to become a likeness of the whole."[46] Thus, "the babbling of a brook" could seem to even an awake individual, as "the voice of a friend" due to the relationship between perception, memory, and imagination.

Coleridge identifies the psychology of perception with a distinction between Reason and Understanding, but not as most moderns use these words. Lewis knew this, and his personal index

[43]Marginalia by Sara Coleridge in Sara Coleridge, *Phantasmion* (London: William Pickering, 1837), 36-37 (Louis Wilson Round Special Collections Library at the University of North Carolina at Chapel Hill); cf. Elizabeth Shand, "Sara Coleridge's Annotated *Phantasmion*: 'Is It Not the Work of a Poet's Daughter if Not of a Poet?,'" *The Coleridge Bulletin* 59 (2002): 13-28.

[44]Marginalia by C. S. Lewis, in Coleridge, *The Friend* (1865), 386 (C. S. Lewis Library collection, Wade).

[45]Coleridge, *The Friend* (1865), 89; cf. *The Friend* (1969), 145.

[46]Coleridge, *The Friend* (1865), 89; cf. *The Friend* (1969), 146.

to *The Friend* highlights Coleridge's distinction between the two. The former is a faculty, as Lewis notes, that "admits of no degrees," is "peculiar to man" yet "common to all men," and "recognises our unity with the whole."[47] The latter, by comparison, is "shared with beasts," "capable of *using* the Reason," and provides "necessary but deceptive creations."[48] Reason is thereby closely associated with divine image-bearing for Coleridge, and Lewis unquestionably tracks Coleridge's meaning on this point, noting marginally in one comment that Reason is "*common* only in the sense of being common to all rational beings."[49]

The key to Coleridge's distinction is a division between human knowledge of both the sensuous and supersensuous. "God, the soul, eternal truth" are the objects of Reason, since Reason is "the organ of the supersensuous." Understanding, by contrast, allows us to "generalize and arrange the phænomena of perception." The upshot is that—unlike animals, which know only material realities—the human person has "the power of acquainting itself with invisible realities or objects."[50] In turn, much as Reason "recognises our unity with the whole," the artistic imagination actively creates that which the soul knows but the rational intellect remains unable fully to grasp. Nature yields data, but imagination fills or "impregnates" the Understanding, allowing the mind to become "intuitive" and "a living power."[51] Thus, dream states represent in narrative that which the discursive intellect cannot conceive: "The common end of all *narrative*, nay, of *all*, Poems is to convert a *series* into a *Whole*:

---

[47]Marginalia by C. S. Lewis, in Coleridge, *The Friend* (1865), 390 (C. S. Lewis Library collection, Wade).

[48]Marginalia by C. S. Lewis, in Coleridge, *The Friend* (1865), 390 (C. S. Lewis Library collection, Wade).

[49]Marginalia by C. S. Lewis, in Coleridge, *The Friend* (1865), 280 (C. S. Lewis Library collection, Wade).

[50]Coleridge, *The Friend* (1865), 96; cf. *The Friend* (1969), 156.

[51]Samuel Taylor Coleridge, *The Statesman's Manual*, in *Lay Sermons*, ed. R. J. White (London: Routledge & Kegan Paul, 1972), 69.

to make those events, which in real or imagined History move in a *strait* Line, assume to our Understandings a *circular* motion—the snake with it's Tail in it's Mouth."[52]

The connection between nature, dream states, and the self should thereby not surprise Lewis's readers. The good story is so satisfying—what Tolkien calls the good catastrophe or "eucatastrophe"—precisely because it articulates the unity and meaning of the whole. In religious terms, the redemptive end of a story is a beatific vision of divine union. Thus, the creative invocation of the dream state signifies not an escape from reality or a childish form of wish fulfillment. Rather, as Douglas Hedley explains, "An encounter with great art confronts the soul with dimensions of reality of which the discursive intellect is often barely aware."[53]

All this figures into our understanding of C. S. Lewis, for I am suggesting that Lewis recognized in Coleridge's thought a path for understanding the relationship between the perceptive self, nature, and story. Lewis's poem "To Roy Campbell" acknowledges this inspiration in the literary tradition that flows not from Rousseau (as commonly believed) but, however paradoxically, from Coleridge. For while Coleridge drew on vastly disparate resources in his thought, he was the one who revived the English regard for awe and wonder: Coleridge "re-discovered the soul's depth and height."[54] Lewis knew that Coleridge had recovered an ancient wisdom, but his calamitous personal life overshadowed his legacy. In a time when empiricism and utilitarianism had benumbed the English-speaking world, Coleridge's renewed attention to self-knowledge, imagination, and higher Reason paved the way for a renewal of faith.

---

[52]Samuel Taylor Coleridge, *The Collected Letters of Samuel Taylor Coleridge*, ed. E. L. Griggs (Oxford: Clarendon, 1956–1971), IV.545 (Coleridge's spelling maintained).

[53]Douglas Hedley, *Living Forms of the Imagination* (London: T&T Clark, 2008), 205.

[54]C. S. Lewis, "To Roy Campbell," in *Poems*, ed. Walter Hooper (New York: Harcourt, Brace & World, 1964), 66.

Symbolic Language

The power of imagination to capture something in language that remains beyond our ability to communicate takes us to one of Lewis's most underappreciated prose writings: "Transposition." Lewis most likely delivered the address on the Feast of Pentecost, June 9, 1946.[55] Nevertheless, while "Transposition" begins with a discussion of the descent of the Holy Spirit at Pentecost, Lewis concentrates on the experience of those who gathered together—on *glossolalia*, or "speaking with tongues"—rather than the divine nature.

The miracle of *glossolalia* had always embarrassed him. For skeptics, the tongues of Pentecost are a marker of religious hysteria, but Lewis suggests that Christians need not reject the biblical account as some sort of pathological disorder. Instead, he compares the description of the tongues at Pentecost to the erotic lexicon employed by many Christian mystics, in which certain familiar expressions may be used to describe both emotional states and some other natural signification.[56]

On this basis, Lewis proposes a robust account of language. He begins by addressing the relationship between physical sensation and emotions, for we often describe our emotions in words that could equally apply to pleasurable or unpleasurable sensations. Thus, an experience of profound satisfaction may be nearly identical to feelings of intense romantic affection or, rather differently, nausea.[57] Introspection is little help. The moment we stop to

---

[55]Contrary to Walter Hooper's dating of the sermon, Smilde convincingly explains that the "Transposition" sermon belongs to Whitsunday 1946 (Arend Smilde, "C. S. Lewis's 'Transposition': Text and Context," *Sehnsucht: The C. S. Lewis Journal* 13 [2019]: 28-56; cf. Hooper, "Introduction," in *The Weight of Glory and Other Addresses* [New York: HarperOne, 2001], 19). The events Hooper associates with "Transposition" more likely belong to his "Ascension" sermon of 1944. I owe a debt of gratitude to Norbert Feinendegen for his expertise in this matter.

[56]C. S. Lewis, "Transposition," in *Weight of Glory and Other Addresses*, 93-94.

[57]Lewis, "Transposition," 96.

consider what is happening emotionally, our minds focus almost entirely on the physical sensation. Nevertheless, we know intuitively that the experience is either pleasurable or painful. Then, Lewis claims that language, for all its limitations, may also be used to describe "higher" and "lower" systems. Physical sensations are "lower" than emotions, if only because the former lack the range of variations of the "higher" form. As a result, we substitute poorer linguistic mediums for richer ones, since the exchange demands that words in a finite system have multiple meanings.[58]

There is a problem in all this, of course. We can only understand the transposition if we are aware of the "higher" medium. Lewis illustrates the problem using the concept of dimensionality—an idea he frequently alludes to in his works. As with Edwin Abbott's *Flatland* (1884), Lewis explains that a two-dimensional creature cannot recognize a three-dimensional world because the idea itself will seem too mysterious and, ultimately, only a figment of the imagination.

The everyday word for a transposition is *symbol*, but Lewis worries that its ordinary use fails to capture the fuller meaning. Some senses of the term work fine, while others fall short; letters and sounds can symbolize for the eye or ear, but a picture remains part of the imaged world rather than the thing itself. For instance, an image of the sun is not sunlight, but the picture does make real sunlight present in some capacity. Lewis explains that this sense of presence distances his use of the term from the use of "symbol" in daily speech; it would be better, he thinks, to use "not symbolical but sacramental" to identify the idea and thereby avoid tenuous notions of some "mere symbolism."[59]

Once again, Lewis is patterning his own thought on the philosophical theology of Samuel Taylor Coleridge. In *The Statesman's Manual*, Coleridge defines the symbol as

---

[58]Lewis, "Transposition," 99.
[59]Lewis, "Transposition," 102-3.

characterized by a translucence of the Special in the Individual or of the General in the Especial or of the Eternal through and in the Temporal. It always partakes of the Reality which it renders intelligible; and while it enunciates the whole, abides itself as a living part in that Unity, of which it is the representative.[60]

The Coleridgean symbol allows that higher realities can appear in finite forms. Linguistically, the symbol differs from analogy, and Coleridge intentionally uses the term *consubstantial* to explain the symbol's relationship to higher orders of being. For this reason, Coleridge's idea bears resemblance to the religious sacrament, and Lewis, likewise, describes the relationship as "sacramental" and a kind of "transubstantiation."[61]

In the "Transposition" sermon, Lewis explains why skeptics might conflate religious experiences with mere nature. The cynic identifies only an apparent deception or some imagined development from nature. To the one who knows only the lower order, no other conclusion is reasonable or even possible. The words of the apostle Paul are profoundly illuminating: "The natural man receiveth not the things of the Spirit of God: for they are foolishness unto him: neither can he know them, because they are spiritually discerned" (1 Cor 2:14).

The Lord's Supper is just this sort of symbol. In *Letters to Malcolm: Chiefly on Prayer* (1964), Lewis addresses the transposition between higher and lower orders as a kind of magic.[62] Against the tendency to understand the relationship between the elements and Christ's own body empirically, Lewis suggests that conceptualizing what happens in the liturgy requires an act of imagination more suited

---

[60]Coleridge, *Statesman's Manual*, 30.
[61]Lewis, "Transposition," 103.
[62]C. S. Lewis, *Letters to Malcolm: Chiefly on Prayer* (San Diego: Harcourt Brace, 1992), 103.

to the reader of fairy tales than the scientist. Think too hard on the divine presence, and one is liable to fall into either abstruse metaphysics or an arbitrary psychology. Instead, Communion testifies of heaven, much as earthly realities testify to the facts of a material universe.[63] In the end, however one conceives of this symbol, Lewis thinks we must never eliminate the overflow of meaning, reducing the sacrament to nature alone. Such inspection "is like taking a red coal out of the fire to examine it: it becomes a dead coal."[64]

The sense of overflow that Lewis identifies in the transpositional symbol guards him against an excessive reliance on feeling or individual experience alone. The symbol isn't a symbol only because I feel it is meaningful. No. While the individual does feel a longing that the symbol captures in part, the symbol also points to something more—a higher reality that language and matter alone can only partly convey.

In this, Lewis tracks closely once again with Coleridge, for whom the symbol provides an "outer" or external form that nourishes and sustains thought. In one sense, the symbol may be identified with an act of sensory perception, as when Coleridge explains, "In looking at objects of Nature while I am thinking, as at yonder moon dim-glimmering thro' the dewy window-pane, I seem rather to be seeking, as it were *asking*, a symbolical language for something within me that already and forever exists, than observing any thing

---

[63]Lewis, *Letters to Malcolm*, 104.

[64]Lewis, *Letters to Malcolm*, 105. Notably, marginal lines appear in Lewis's copy of Griffiths's *The Golden String* in an evocative passage on the Eucharist: "In an instant everything was changed. Our gifts had been taken into the hands of Christ; they had been blessed and consecrated, and now they had been transformed into him. The earthly elements had been transfigured, and by this transfiguration all human labour had been given a new meaning. By being offered to God under the signs of the bread and the wine, it had been taken up into the sacrifice of Christ. It had been sanctified by him and made part of his own sacrifice for the salvation of the world. By this all human labour had been made sacred, because it had been brought into relation with the labour of Christ for man's salvation" (marginalia in Bede Griffiths, *The Golden String* [London: Harvill, 1954], 142 [C. S. Lewis Library collection, Wade]).

new."[65] Yet, in another sense, the mind also requires external symbols that point to the supersensuous reality for which the mind truly longs, since "the soul [is] sensible of its imperfection in itself, of its *Halfness*. . . . It cannot *think* without a symbol—neither can it *live* without something that is to be at once its Symbol, & its *Other half*."[66]

The driving difference between Lewis and Coleridge here is more a matter of emphasis than logic. For Coleridge, the post-Kantian turn was full of possibility and promise, allowing that a language of symbols could capture the mind's longing for union: "I am not a God, that I should stand alone."[67] For Lewis, the post-Feuerbachian world required attentiveness to the potential pitfalls of symbolic language and an awareness of the ways that the human search for meaning could go astray: never follow individual experience as the measure of all things.[68]

NARRATIVE PRESENCE

Understanding Lewis on symbol and sacrament allows readers to return once again to his powerful discussion of the RAF officer's interruption in *Mere Christianity*. Lewis's response to the man, beginning with an affirmation of his experience, paired with a caution against the sort of tangled thinking that leads to falsehood, depends on an appeal to alterity or otherness. The reason a map of the ocean proves effective in sailing across the Atlantic is precisely that it takes the experiences of so many different mariners into account. Similarly, theology matters in an exposition of Christian faith—and,

---

[65]Samuel Taylor Coleridge, *The Notebooks of Samuel Taylor Coleridge*, ed. Kathleen Coburn et al. (Princeton, NJ: Princeton University Press, 1957–2002), II.2546.
[66]Coleridge, *Notebooks*, III.3325.
[67]Coleridge, *Notebooks*, III.3325. Modiano explains, "While inner symbols might sustain some form of mental or imaginative activity, outer symbols alone sustain the soul and life itself. The outer symbols provide what the mind can never have or achieve by itself, namely the means of perfecting itself through union with an external object and, in more ordinary terms, companionship" (Raimonda Modiano, *Coleridge and the Concept of Nature* [Tallahassee: Florida State University Press, 1985], 73).
[68]Lewis, *Mere Christianity*, 11.

VIRGINIA WOOLF

Her Art as a Novelist

BY

JOAN BENNETT, M.A.
University Lecturer in English

CAMBRIDGE
AT THE UNIVERSITY PRESS
1945

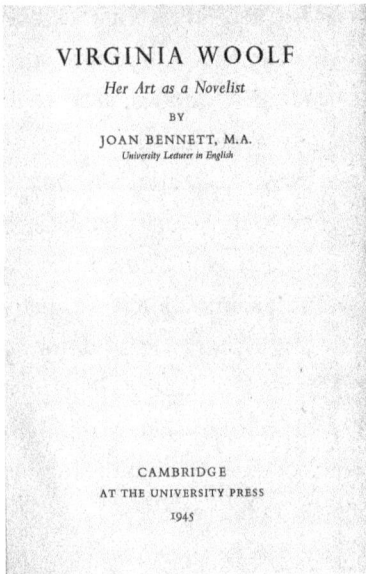

Figure 3.8. Joan Bennett, *Virginia Woolf, Her Art as a Novelist*

here, Lewis could just as easily have referenced church traditions or the creeds—because the witness of the past can both affirm the legitimacy of our experiences of God and, simultaneously, correct them. Many popular ideas today are only old ones previously discarded: "To believe in the popular religion of modern England is retrogression—like believing the earth is flat."[69]

For Lewis, sacraments such as baptism and the Lord's Supper provide what Coleridge calls "outness," but he also thinks that narrative functions in a similarly sacramental manner. At the front of Joan Bennett's *Virginia Woolf: Her Art as a Novelist*, published just one year before Lewis first delivered his sermon, we find a remarkable precis in Lewis's own hand of the "Transposition" essay:

1. Different (even opposite) states of consciousness can reveal to introspection the same physical thrill.

2. A similar principle is discovered elsewhere, e.g. different letters [and] sounds can be represented by [the] same letters: different parts of [an] orchestra by [the] same notes. In drawing different 3-dim forms can be represented by same 2-dim figure.

3. Suggestion. Psycho-physical symbolism, or, in general, that "Higher" & "Lower" mean symbolised & symbol.

---

[69]Lewis, *Mere Christianity*, 155.

4. But a special kind of symbol: not like arithmetic[,] nor like algebra, but like Drawing, i.e. Transposition.

5. Three cases. (a) Where we know both (b) where we fully know one & have an obscure knowledge of the other. (c) where we know only one.

6. Our example in 1. Drawing. Spelling.

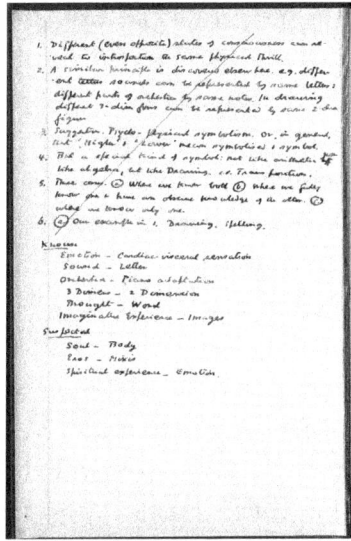

This first part (above) is crossed out by a single diagonal line. Then, in what follows, we see Lewis

Figure 3.9. Marginalia by C. S. Lewis in Bennett, *Virginia Woolf*

drawing out the distinction between "known" and "suspected" orders of transposition:

Known
    Emotion—Cardiac-visceral sensation
    Sound—Letter
    Orchestra—Piano adaptation
    3 Dimens—2 Dimension
    Thought—Word
    Imaginative Experience—Images

Suspected
    Soul—Body
    Eros—Mixis
    Spiritual experience—Emotion.[70]

---

[70]*Mixis* is the verb for "mixing" in Greek; marginalia by C. S. Lewis, in Joan Bennett, *Virginia Woolf: Her Art as a Novelist* (Cambridge: Cambridge University Press, 1945), front pastedown (C. S. Lewis Library collection, Wade).

It is not hard to see Lewis working out the central ideas of the "Transposition" sermon in these marginalia. Still, readers may rightly ask, what gave rise to this reflection in the first place?

In fact, a series of marginal lines that appear within the same book may furnish some insight. Bennett describes Woolf's practice of signifying different states of consciousness in six character-types within her novels. This "subjective element" in her stories allows readers to understand universal human experiences: "He is attending to what it feels like to be young, or middle aged, or old; to be in the country or at school or in a London street; to rejoice, or to suffer, to strive or to be serene. The six personalities, with their differences of temperament, are the vehicles by which the experience is brought to him."[71] Elsewhere, in a passage marginally lined by Lewis, the relationship between the characters and states of consciousness is connected to the artistry of the author who, through a "command of poetic language" that requires a Coleridgean "willing suspension of disbelief," enables the reader to understand the self through the form of the story.[72]

Stories, for Lewis, provide the opportunity for the individual to engage in imaginative acts of sympathy. The symbol-making capacity of the mind allows readers to see beyond the self, through the imagination, and engage the surplus of meaning in and through the narrative symbol of the other. Thus, in his *Experiment in Criticism*, Lewis extols the power of reading to allow readers to explore the belief and imagination of even those unlike us—whether Thomas Carlyle, D. H. Lawrence, or, were it possible, the scribblings of a dog: "In reading great literature I become a thousand

---

[71]Marginal underline in Joan Bennett, *Virginia Woolf*, 35 (C. S. Lewis Library collection, Wade).

[72]Marginal lining in Joan Bennett, *Virginia Woolf*, 108 (C. S. Lewis Library collection, Wade).

men and yet remain myself. . . . I transcend myself; and am never more myself than when I do."[73]

The discovery of Lewis's marginalia in Bennett's *Virginia Woolf* deepens the significance of narrative within this powerful sermon. Midway through the sermon, Lewis begins telling the fable of a woman who bears a son while locked in a dungeon. The boy, raised by his mother in the confines of their cell, has never known a world beyond the darkness of those walls.[74] So to teach her son of the glorious places beyond the cell, the woman draws images of the outer world that the boy cannot know, including mountains, rivers, and other features of the landscape. One day, to her complete astonishment, the mother realizes that, despite all her efforts, her son does not fully understand. Despite all her efforts, the child cannot fully grasp that the "real world" is, in a sense, "less visible" than the landscape his mother creates and thus, truly, more visible than he can yet imagine.[75]

This is what makes autobiography, conversion narratives, and other life writings so powerful: through the narration of a life, we encounter the other and begin to see the world through their eyes. For Lewis, as with Coleridge, narrative participates in the real sacramentally. Narrative partakes in the reality it renders intelligible to the reader, enunciating the whole "as a living part in that Unity, of which it is the representative."[76] Lewis cannot help but worry that such stories will inevitably be "suffocatingly subjective," but he cannot help but rely on them, too, in the hope that through such an encounter we will begin to understand a common—even universal—experience, the uncanny experience wherein one

---

[73]C. S. Lewis, *An Experiment in Criticism* (Cambridge: Cambridge University Press, 1961), 141.

[74]Lewis, "Transposition," 109.

[75]Lewis, "Transposition," 110.

[76]Coleridge, *Statesman's Manual*, 30.

exclaims, "What! Have *you* felt that too? I always thought I was the only one."[77]

Nevertheless, the mind longs for that which even the words of the most powerful story cannot fully realize. I think this is one of the reasons Lewis's wardrobe has a perennial hold over visitors to the Marion E. Wade Center. In standing before Lewis's own wardrobe—what might otherwise be regarded as a finely crafted but otherwise ordinary piece of furniture—the reader of the Chronicles of Narnia moves from narrative symbol into a physical embodiment of a world created by imagination. The substance of the imagined thing brings us closer in transposition, by a lower approach, to the ideal. This is, for much the same reason, why the Eucharist remains among the highest symbols of faith for Lewis, for there at the table we encounter the living God in a wondrous moment of holiness.

Beholding the Light

Here we might be content to conclude this study of the ways Romanticism permeates Lewis's life and writings. I have not only examined references to the great poet-philosophers of the early nineteenth century in his works but also sought the deeper Romantic logic that is woven into the fabric of Lewis's thought. In this chapter alone, such an analysis has required attentiveness to his understanding of nature, dream states, symbols, and narrative. In all this, we are reminded repeatedly that, for Lewis, Romanticism names a longing for which the created order seems ever-unable fully to express.

To see this clearly, we must turn finally to his great work, "The Weight of Glory," which was first preached at the University Church of St. Mary the Virgin, Oxford, in June 1941. The sermon

---

[77]Lewis, *Surprised by Joy: The Shape of My Early Life* (Boston: Mariner, 2012), vii.

demonstrates, once again, Lewis's indebtedness to the British Romantics. Both overt and subtle references to Wordsworth, Keats, and Shelley abound in the text, and Lewis notes, once again, that Romanticism is the familiar name for that "desire for our own far-off country" to which he aspires.[78]

Romanticism runs deeper still, for Lewis describes an idea that we seldom find discussed with such capacious power: the numinous.[79] Since heaven lies *beyond* our experience, we must always rely on descriptions from *within* our experience. In Wordsworth's poetry, to take but one example Lewis mentions, the poet returns to memories ("spots of time"), only to discover the limits of even those moments: "It was not *in* them, it only came *through* them, and what came through them was longing."[80] We intend these reminiscences to draw us into union with the divine, but they necessarily fall short. We may mistake the "spot of time" for the thing itself, but memories are only messengers.

Nature is the obvious choice. Scripture sanctions it. Participating in Nature's beauty, we find ourselves longing for the numinous even more. It isn't beauty, per se, that we seek; it's something more than language can contain: "to be united with the beauty we see, to pass into it, to receive it into ourselves, to bathe in it, to become part of it."[81] For just this reason, tales abound in ancient and modern times of fairies, nymphs, and all sorts of heavenly beings. Nevertheless, these stories only image what nature provides. The state of longing—the sort of "vision in a dream" we find in "Kubla Khan" or *The Great Divorce*—reminds us that the stuff of earth may

---

[78]C. S. Lewis, "The Weight of Glory," in *Weight of Glory*, 29.

[79]Evidence in Lewis's marginalia suggests that he follows Rudolf Otto in the belief that Schleiermacher and other Romantics were responsible for the "rediscovery" of the *sensus numinous* (see Lewis's personal copy of Otto's *Religious Essays*, 72 and personal index on verso of rear free endpaper [C. S. Lewis Library collection, Wade]).

[80]Lewis, "Weight of Glory," 30.

[81]Lewis, "Weight of Glory," 42.

participate in a higher reality. Soul and body, eros and *mixis*, spiritual experience and emotion. Each transposition prompts us to
recall that the sensible experiences of this life are signposts for
higher realities, for our pleasures are remnants of divine energies,
"implanted in matter when He made the worlds."[82] In the meantime,
we wait in expectation.

Understanding this helps to explain why so often Lewis appeals to the numinous in fiction. Perhaps the best single example appears near the end of *The Voyage of the Dawn Treader*,
when the vessel has traveled many windless days, even to the
end of the known world.[83] There is water to drink and flowers
in abundance in a lilied sea that seems to partake in an un-
natural vitality.[84] Then, as the children's journey comes to a
close, the chivalrous mouse Reepicheep bids his companions
goodbye, casts his sword into the sea, and paddles off to the
mountains beyond.[85]

In fact, similar visions and mystical reports of the numinous
appear repeatedly across Lewis's fictional works. In *The Great Divorce*, Lewis portrays glory in the chorus of birds and beasts and
angels singing in the rising sun.[86] In *The Last Battle*, when the
children have traveled less than an hour or perhaps many years,
they finally discover themselves in a place "more real and more
beautiful than the Narnia outside the Stable door!"[87] And at the end
of book two of the Space Trilogy, *Perelandra*, the numinous is en-
visioned in the Great Dance, where a procession of entities appear
as cords intersecting in a luminosity of beings, truths, and universal
qualities, "more ecstatic" and "more intense, as dimension was

[82]Lewis, "Weight of Glory," 44.
[83]C. S. Lewis, *The Voyage of the Dawn Treader* (London: William Collins, 1952), 177.
[84]Lewis, *Dawn Treader*, 177, 180.
[85]Lewis, *Dawn Treader*, 184-85.
[86]Lewis, *Great Divorce*, 145.
[87]C. S. Lewis, *The Last Battle* (New York: Collier, 1970), 179-80.

added to dimension" until his own intellection faded behind the "zenith of complexity."[88] Each points to the persistent notion that something higher lies beyond even the highest capacities of human imagination.

What are we to do in the meantime? "The Weight of Glory" is clear: love. Love your neighbor, not as an object or as a means to an end, but as a deep symbol—one who participates in that which lies beyond our comprehension: "It is a serious thing to live in a society of possible gods and goddesses."[89] To give true honor to the divine beyond our comprehension, we must return to the most ordinary and commonplace. For even as an act so simple as eating bread and sipping wine draws us into communion with God, so care for one's neighbor is true service to Christ: "Next to the Blessed Sacrament itself, your neighbour is the holiest object presented to your senses."[90]

BEGINNING AND ENDING

In the final book of Wordsworth's *Prelude*, the poet describes his ascent of Mount Snowdon in northern Wales. Moving with an eager pace, in silence, he reaches the top and sees the moon, "naked in the Heavens":

> I found myself of a huge sea of mist,
> Which meek and silent, rested at my feet.
> A hundred hills their dusky backs upheaved
> All over this still Ocean, and beyond . . .[91]

The sight of the landscape below reveals the power of poetic imagination, unifying the whole. It is a powerful moment. The lines that follow, however, make clear that nature's power comes to fullness

---

[88]C. S. Lewis, *Perelandra: A Novel* (New York: Scribner, 2003), 187-88.
[89]Lewis, "Weight of Glory," 45.
[90]Lewis, "Weight of Glory," 46.
[91]Wordsworth, *The Prelude* (1805), book 13.43-46, in *Wordsworth's Poetry and Prose*, 367.

in the "meditation" that "rose in me that night / . . . when the scene / Had passed away."[92]

What does Wordsworth discover? Love.

> From love, for here
> Do we begin and end, all grandeur comes,
> All truth and beauty, from pervading love,
> That gone, we are as dust.[93]

Love, Wordsworth explains, accompanies imagination. Nature and imagination draw us into love: love for his sister, Dorothy; love for his wife, Mary; love for his friend Coleridge. All spring, in turns throughout his narrative, from "The feeling of life endless, the one thought / By which we live, Infinity and God."[94]

In his appeal to love, Lewis reveals himself as a co-laborer with the British Romantics before him. While some may worry that his emphasis on the personal places too great a weight on feeling and individual experience, Lewis's writings repeatedly demonstrate that human imagination may point to higher realities than we recognize by sensory knowledge alone. In describing the sublime waterfall, writing the personal narrative, and reading the fairy tale, we seek the fullness of truths we have already begun to intuit as bearers of the image of God. In the meantime, we love even as we see darkly, for "To know that one is dreaming is to be no longer perfectly asleep."[95]

---

[92]Wordsworth, *The Prelude* (1805), book 13.66-68, in *Wordsworth's Poetry and Prose*, 367.
[93]Wordsworth, *The Prelude* (1805), book 13.149-52, in *Wordsworth's Poetry and Prose*, 369-70.
[94]Wordsworth, *The Prelude* (1805), book 13.183-84, in *Wordsworth's Poetry and Prose*, 370. So, too, for Coleridge, for whom the love of God is known in and through the other: "The best, the truly lovely, in each & all is God. Therefore the truly Beloved is the symbol of God to whomever it is truly beloved by!" (Coleridge, *Notebooks*, II.2540).
[95]Lewis, *Four Loves*, 180.

RESPONSE
Keith L. Johnson

Professor Barbeau's book is in many ways the fulfillment of Clyde
Kilby's dream. This legendary Wheaton College professor dreamed
of creating an enduring space at the college that could provide
American evangelicals with resources to help them overcome the
aesthetic and intellectual poverty of twentieth-century fundamen-
talism. The writings of C. S. Lewis helped turn Kilby's dream into
a reality. Kilby recognized the very trait Professor Barbeau has
highlighted in this book: Lewis's writings possess transformative
power because they connect his readers' shared human experiences,
desires, fears, and longings to their faith in God.

Yet this very trait also has been the source of controversy about
Lewis's theology. Professor Barbeau's discussion of Morris Inch's
critique of Lewis serves as a case in point. Professor Inch worried
that Lewis's theology was mired in subjectivity and undermined
the objective truth of God. After all, if we begin with our own subjective experience and then reflect on that experience to draw conclusions about God, how can we be sure that our description of
God is anything other than a description of our own experience?
How can we know that our picture of God is anything other than a
giant picture of ourselves? That would be idolatry, the act of making
God in our own creaturely image.

This critique frames the central question Professor Barbeau has
been answering throughout this book: Did C. S. Lewis allow human
subjectivity to determine his account of God and the Christian life?
Did Lewis fall into this idolatrous trap? Professor Barbeau has
shown that the answer to each of these questions is no. He has
convincingly demonstrated that C. S. Lewis's description of God is

not confined within the limits of his own human subjectivity. Lewis's critical appropriation of the Romantic tradition gave him the conceptual and theological tools he needed to write narratives that both connect with our shared experiences *and* remain faithful to the God who always remains other than us. Indeed, Lewis is rightly seen as the last of the Romantics. He was at once a sympathetic student and an incisive critic of the Romantic tradition, in part because he saw firsthand how quickly the Romantic optimism of the nineteenth century flowed into the bloody trenches of the twentieth. And when he faced his own spiritual and personal battles and then shared them with the world, he did so by brilliantly refining what he learned from the Romantics about our shared experience without suffocating on his own subjectivity.

Professor Barbeau has demonstrated that, through both their failures and successes, the Romantics taught Lewis how to write stories that connect with our lived experience but direct our gaze to God rather than ourselves. This argument culminates in this chapter's discussion of Lewis's sacramental imagination. Professor Barbeau shows that Lewis recognized that the natural world, and our experience of it, is not an end itself; it is a sign, a representation of the true and hidden reality that lies beyond what we can see and know directly. Christians have eyes to see this reality only by faith, because they can recognize truths from their experience *as* true because they were first announced and explained by the prior action of the God who remains ever beyond creaturely life. If humans begin with God, they can look at the world around us and see God at work in every part of their lives. And this insight gives them compelling and imaginative stories to tell.

I think Professor Barbeau's argument stands as a tremendous achievement. He has offered a sophisticated and brilliant reading of Lewis's work. But more significantly, he has placed the writings of C. S. Lewis in their theological, historical, and philosophical context and shown how this context informs not only our reading of Lewis but also the viability of Kilby's dream about how Lewis's work might contribute to the future of American evangelicalism. This book serves as an excellent example of how fresh archival work can bring new insights about the most familiar of texts.

While I do not have concerns about Professor Barbeau's interpretation of Lewis, I do have reservations about Lewis's approach itself. I'll focus on the prior chapter's culminating argument. Professor Barbeau argued that Lewis utilized universal human experiences in his writings without falling into the trap of subjectivism because he viewed the natural world as a symbol of higher realties, as a sacrament. Here I would like to pause, because whenever I hear someone talk about the world being *sacramental*, I want to ask that person to be more concrete and specific. A sacrament is by definition a sign of some other reality. And in the Christian doctrine of the sacraments, that reality is a specific and particular *person*. The word *sacrament* comes from the Latin *sacramentum*, which is a translation of the Greek word *mystērion*, "mystery." And in the New Testament, this word is always associated with the saving work of Jesus Christ. Think, for example, of Ephesians 1:8-10: "With all wisdom and insight [God] has made known to us the *mystery* of his will, according to his good pleasure that he set forth in Christ, as a plan for the fullness of time, to gather up all things in him, things in heaven and things on earth" (NRSV). The mystery of God's will, the *sacramentum*, is revealed to us in Jesus Christ; he is the one who determines the meaning of all things in heaven and earth—including our experience of these things.

The centrality of Jesus is why Protestants generally limit the sacraments to those church practices associated directly with the example and command of Jesus: baptism and the Lord's Supper. And it is significant that these two practices are directly connected to the story of the death and resurrection of Jesus, the gospel. This is why the Protestant Reformers insisted so strongly that Word and sacrament always be held together. The sacraments point to Jesus, but they cannot be understood or received rightly apart from the faith that comes by hearing the Word about Jesus, the gospel. This faith requires a prior encounter with Jesus himself as the risen Lord, and an answer to the question he finally poses to everyone: "Who do you say that I am?"

In short, the content of the sacrament is Jesus himself, and our knowledge of the sacrament's meaning depends on our prior hearing of the gospel and our faithful response to Jesus as our Lord. In my admittedly limited reading of Lewis, I worry that he is not always concrete and specific in his appeals to symbolic and sacramental realities. His writings leave things far more open, and his stories paint a picture of God and our relationship with him that is a bit fuzzy around the edges. I find myself wanting Lewis to say more about God, and to say these things more precisely, so that his readers cannot escape the conclusion that any divine words we discern in the created realities around us are the words of none other than the crucified and risen Jesus himself.

For this reason, I am not convinced that Lewis's writings will actually provide the solution to the aesthetic and intellectual poverty of evangelicalism in the way Clyde Kilby hoped so many years ago. But that doesn't mean Professor Kilby's efforts were in vain, because I know someone who does fit this vision. It is Professor Barbeau himself—a sympathetic yet critical reader of the Romantics, a loving mentor who connects with his students right where they are, and a faithful teacher who day after day points everyone around him to Jesus. All of these traits have been visible in this book, and for that I am grateful.

CONCLUSION

IF I WERE C. S. LEWIS, I suppose I'd conclude this book with a vast, fugal vision that draws readers into the eternal dance of the triune God. Since I'm not, I'll take just a moment to offer a few thoughts on the astute observations of my three respondents. I'll also answer a question that came up when I first delivered the "C. S. Lewis and the Romantic Imagination" lectures.

A PATH WORTH TRAVELING

Dr. Sarah Borden's response to my first chapter, "C. S. Lewis and the 'Romantic Heresy,'" provides an engaging philosophical exploration of perhaps *the* pivotal question of the modern period: "How do we know things to be true?" Her response teases out some of the ways that phenomenologists such as Husserl and Heidegger approached these vital issues. Yet her appeal to Augustine for further insight shows that, in many ways, the modern question is also a rather ancient one. Sorting this out will, indeed, take considerable work, and I'm grateful to have Dr. Borden as a colleague in this endeavor.

As she notes, the phenomenologists are themselves heirs of the Enlightenment- and Romantic-era philosophers and theologians who came before them. This includes, of course, the great Romantic poets, who contributed uniquely to the ways these topics were addressed in their own times. The questions these authors raised about the so-called objective and subjective dominated some circles (particularly on the Continent), so it is no surprise that those who came after them shed new light on the problem.

Dr. Borden's response contributes several helpful linguistic distinctions. Sustained reflection on the differences between, say, sensory knowledge gained by the sight of a bird or the taste of a cake and the emotional response to an encounter with the numinous can go a long way toward clarifying what we might mean by the personal, the subjective, or even such fraught religious terms as *feeling* and *intuition*. In this, I wholeheartedly agree with Dr. Borden that the question Christians should ask is not, "How do we get the subjective *out* of our objective claims?" but, as she states, "How and on the basis of *which aspects of* each of our subjective, personal experiences can one make responsible, evidenced truth claims?" In some respects, I think this sort of distinction (though certainly implied in such works as *Mere Christianity* and *The Abolition of Man*) shows that some aspects of the twentieth-century conversation simply weren't within Lewis's purview. Nevertheless, he was certainly attuned to language and, I suspect, would have appreciated the phenomenological assist that Dr. Borden and other philosophers might offer.

Uniquely religious concerns certainly complicate the matter. In Lewis's works, the various contributions to the Wheaton College faculty debate, and Dr. Borden's own response to my chapter, topics such as biblical inspiration and authority, church traditions, the universality of reason, and the impact of sin on personal experience each contribute to and invariably shape the argument. Inch's cautionary remarks against Romantic "subjectivity"—initiated by Clyde Kilby's defense of the imagination no less than Lewis's apologetics—remind us that, for him, nothing less than the universal truth of the Bible (and Christianity) was at stake.

For this reason, I suspect Lewis would be far more amenable than Morris Inch to Sarah Borden's belief that objective truth can only be accessed by way of "personal, subjective experience." There's ample evidence that the Reformers and other early inheritors of

Protestantism might even have agreed, too. But even today we may discover that—whether in the poetry and prose of the nineteenth century or the sundry writings of Lewis—a favorable valuation of feeling, emotions, and personal experience in matters of Christian faith continues to induce fierce opposition. Nevertheless, as Dr. Borden notes, this is "a path well worth traveling."

THE COMPLEXITY OF SUBJECTIVITY

In response to my second chapter, "C. S. Lewis and the Anxiety of Memory," Dr. Matthew Lundin focuses on the historical. I'm glad to know that he shares my enthusiasm for unique archival discoveries! In the Congdon diary, the reader finds the particular writ large. There's nothing fancy about the journal of a young woman in nineteenth-century New York, but there *is* something else that we recover in such an artifact from an earlier age: the particulars of a concrete life that might otherwise be lost to history.

Dr. Lundin recognizes in both Congdon and Lewis something I had nearly overlooked. For me, the two are held together by shared literary practices and a common (if unexpected) spiritual heritage. I was struck by the ways that a young, unknown, and relatively uneducated woman wrote about her life in a manner that shared so much with a mature, famous, and highly educated man. Dr. Lundin points out something else. In life writing, the distinct experience of an individual reveals not only the uniqueness of each person but also the shared muddle that is human existence. To read a diary or a journal is an act of recognition: "to acknowledge the complexity of human subjectivity—and the incarnational truth that God meets us in the midst of our particular, embodied contexts, with all their uncertainty and unresolved tension."

This connection between the general and the particular is illuminating for our understanding of Lewis's own use of life writing in apologetics. As Dr. Lundin notes, Lewis wrote in a time when skepticism toward such an argument was rising, and yet he persisted in order to show others that what holds all people together is a peculiar longing that he called "joy." Lewis's simultaneous embrace of the particular and commitment to a kind of abstraction of the self from context allowed him to speak of both the personal and the universal. I suspect this is one of the reasons Lewis's *Surprised by Joy* continues to enjoy a strong readership. For while some of his examples can feel dated or distant to the reader—whether in his early reading selections or his experiences at boarding school—he touches on something of significance to people from all walks of life.

Worry persists. Much as with Dr. Borden, Dr. Lundin reminds us that dependence on "feeling" can go dramatically wrong. Mention of Nazi propagandist Joseph Goebbels is enough to send even the most dyed-in-the-wool Romanticist running for the nearest intellectual exit. But he also notes that, far from such excesses, Lewis's focus on the particular seems entirely distant from the "unhinged self-assertion" of his contemporaries. Rather, all is "mundane" and "ordinary" and "hemmed in."

THE DIAGRAM OF LOVE

The emphasis on grace that concludes Dr. Lundin's response—of a God who becomes human, rather than a man who strives to become a god—comes through particularly in the theological response by Dr. Keith Johnson to my third chapter, "C. S. Lewis and the Sacramental Imagination." Dr. Johnson recognizes that part of what makes Lewis so attractive to readers is his uncanny ability to connect with them personally. His writings show how "shared human experiences, desires, fears, and longings" relate to the faith they have in God. In this, Lewis is both a recipient of the Romantic tradition and something of a critic.

Dr. Johnson has reminded me that part of what makes Lewis's concept of "joy" or *Sehnsucht* function is not merely the sense of longing after the numinous but the work of the God who made all. If we focus only on what's happening within us, we might lose sight of the one who made the signs we discover along the way. But while these symbols are gifts from "the God who remains ever beyond creaturely life," I think Lewis, like Augustine, might have appealed to the restless heart set right as a sign of just such an encounter.

As with each of the other respondents, Dr. Johnson offers a warning. The events of the twentieth century—events Lewis knew well, not only intellectually but personally—loom large in Dr. Johnson's vision, but his bigger concern is for the association of *symbols* with the *sacramental*. He explains that the sacraments, after all, are really about "a specific and particular *person.*"

The discomfort with the Romantic concept of symbol (one that I maintain Lewis relies on) leads Dr. Johnson to charge him with a lack of focus on Jesus Christ. Lewis leaves us with stories that "paint a picture of God and our relationship with him that is a bit fuzzy around the edges." Gospel witness is, inadvertently, left to the side.

I hardly think Dr. Johnson intends to besmirch the creator of Aslan with careless disregard for Jesus, but I do think he points out something that I, too, had long supposed. Apart from a few famous passages, Lewis doesn't often dwell on Jesus in either fiction or nonfiction works. In some writings, I thought, perhaps Christ vanishes almost entirely from view.

Then, just recently, I was reading through *The Four Loves* with my students. As we progressed through the book, I found myself reflecting on this very question: Where is Jesus in this portrait of love? Almost always I've understood the christological aspect in that work as muted, displayed predominantly in terms of sacrificial love or other meditations on the godlikeness we associate with *agapē*. But then one passage late in the book leaped out before my eyes, as if I'd read it for the very first time:

He creates the universe, already foreseeing . . . the buzzing
cloud of flies about the cross, the flayed back pressed against
the uneven stake, the nails driven through the mesial nerves,
the repeated incipient suffocation as the body droops, the
repeated torture of back and arms as it is time after time, for
breath's sake, hitched up. . . . Herein is love. This is the di-
agram of Love Himself, the inventor of all loves.[1]

How many times had I read this passage on charity and skimmed
over Lewis's profound vision of love and the cross? Yet here it was,
with Lewis describing how, before the creation of the world, the
work of atonement was visibly on display: *agapē* love manifest in
the God who dies for all. Regrettably, if Christ is absent from these
chapters, the fault is mine.

On the other hand, perhaps Lewis's association with the Romantics allows us to see something else we might overlook. For
while Dr. Johnson rightly calls us to attend to the incarnate Word,
the Romantic appeal to the personal directs fresh attention to the
work of the Holy Spirit. If Lewis depends on the God who meets us
in personal experience, the transformed heart, and our encounter
with God in nature, then one might say that Lewis demonstrates a
rather acute awareness of the work of the Holy Spirit. Perhaps Lewis
belongs more to the so-called century of the Spirit than we have
hitherto realized, and, in this, we rediscover a deep-seated trinitarianism in his writings, inviting us to join in the great dance of God.

CHRISTIANITY AND TRUTH

Finally, one question from an attendee has remained with me ever
since my first lecture, namely, Where does my reading place
Lewis in the Anglican tradition? My argument in these pages, focused on the British Romantics, has appealed repeatedly to the

---

[1]C. S. Lewis, *The Four Loves* (New York: HarperCollins, 1960), 162-63.

significance of Samuel Taylor Coleridge for C. S. Lewis's thought. As Lewis surely understood, Coleridge is the most significant Anglican theologian between John Wesley and John Henry Newman. Yet, unlike either Wesley or Newman, Coleridge had relatively few disciples and never established a formal school.

Instead, Coleridge's disparate theological legacy is most often associated with the broad church movement in England. Thomas Arnold, Julius Hare, and F. D. Maurice were all attentive readers of Coleridge's works, drawing from his ideas in the formation of a churchmanship that favored toleration for theological and liturgical diversity within the wide Anglican communion.[2] While the broad church had largely dissipated as a formal movement by the end of the nineteenth century, their critical, literary view of Scripture, embrace of modern science, and broadly tolerant approach to ritual were enfolded into the fabric of the Church of England.

Although Lewis's theological and moral conservatism do not fit entirely well with such a liberal theological perspective, my work in these chapters suggests a shared heritage. Coleridge's well-known aphorism in *Aids to Reflection* (1825) served as something of a touchstone for the movement: "He, who begins by loving Christianity better than Truth, will proceed by loving his own Sect or Church better than Christianity, and end in loving himself better than all."[3] The statement, eminently quotable, fits well with Lewis, too, and could have easily served as a motto for *Mere Christianity*.

In fact, as these chapters have demonstrated, Lewis recognized Coleridge's consequence in modern Anglican thought. A vertical line in the margin of his personal copy of Matthew Arnold's *St. Paul and Protestantism* appears alongside a passage on the "great

---

[2]Tod E. Jones, *The Broad Church; A Biography of a Movement* (Lanham, MD: Lexington Books, 2003).
[3]Samuel Taylor Coleridge, *Aids to Reflection*, ed. John Beer (Princeton, NJ: Princeton University Press, 1993), 107.

Coleridgean position," offering a tantalizing clue to Lewis's own
recognition of an Anglicanism that sought theological clarity
devoid of dogmatism:

> The "great Coleridgian position," that apart from all question
> of the evidence for miracles and of the historical quality of the
> Gospel narratives, the essential matters of Christianity are
> necessary and eternal facts of nature or truths of reason, is
> henceforth the key to the whole defence of Christianity.
> When a Christian virtue is presented to us as obligatory, the
> first thing, therefore, to be asked, is whether our need of it is
> a fact of nature.[4]

While I doubt very much that either Coleridge or Lewis would
embrace Arnold's rather skeptical presentation of this position,
the broad church tradition that flourished in the nineteenth century
owes much to what might be called Coleridge's broadly "human-
istic" thought—that is, a conception of the human that (finding its
roots in the Renaissance) emphasizes our continuity rather than
discontinuity with God.[5]

Lewis, as with Coleridge and the broad church before him, also
shares a profound interest in the ways we construct theological language. Consider his curious treatment of the atonement in book two
of *Mere Christianity*. Early on, Lewis refutes the commonplace notion
that commitment to a single theory of the atonement is essential for
Christian belief. Then, after reviewing various theories (including an
Anselmian theology of substitution), Lewis closes the chapter with

---

[4]Marginalia in Matthew Arnold, *St. Paul and Protestantism: With Other Essays* (London:
Smith, Elder, 1892), 157 (C. S. Lewis Library collection, Wade). The same passage is highlighted in Lewis's personal index at the end of the volume.

[5]For example, consider Douglas Hedley's discussion of Coleridge's Christian humanism
by way of the Cambridge Platonists in "Cudworth, Coleridge, and Schelling," *The
Coleridge Bulletin: The Journal of the Friends of Coleridge* 16 (2000): 63-70; see also Alan
Jacobs, *The Year of Our Lord 1943: Christian Humanism in an Age of Crisis* (New York:
Oxford University Press, 2018).

what appears to be a mere shrug of the shoulders, recommending that readers ignore the issue entirely if they find it unhelpful.[6] For a long time, I thought this was just a bit of coy rhetoric designed to win over a cynical audience, but what if Lewis's shrug actually tells us something significant about his own theological commitments?

Once again, Coleridge may provide a clue to help solve the riddle. In an extended treatment of the atonement and biblical language in *Aids to Reflection* (1825), Coleridge explains how theological metaphors "illustrate a something less known by a partial identification of it with some other thing better understood."[7] Thus, while we find that Saint Paul uses several different metaphors to describe the atoning work of Christ (such as a debt paid, reconciliation, etc.), the causative act remains a mystery. For this reason, Paul describes the atonement in a way that will make sense to his audience, namely, with reference to the *consequences* of the act (thus, Christ's atoning work is *like* the experience of reconciliation between a parent and a wayward child). If we identify Lewis as a Christian formed within the Coleridgean theological tradition, his vision of "mere" Christianity suddenly takes on a new significance.

Of course, identifying church parties is notoriously difficult, and several camps have claimed Lewis over the years. As I explained in the first chapter, the current favor that Lewis enjoys among evangelical Anglicans was not always universal (certainly not in the United States), but his focus on individual faith and historic orthodoxy and relative silence on matters of church polity all contribute to the strong reputation he enjoys among them. Likewise, as Mark Noll has demonstrated, Roman Catholics in America were among his earliest devotees.[8] Nevertheless, there are good reasons

---

[6]C. S. Lewis, *Mere Christianity* (New York: HarperOne, 2000).
[7]Coleridge, *Aids to Reflection*, 318-19.
[8]Mark A. Noll, *C. S. Lewis in America: Readings and Reception, 1935–1947* (Downers Grove, IL: IVP Academic, 2023).

to believe that many of Lewis's theological and liturgical views do not fit well with either the evangelical Anglicans or Anglo-Catholics. His lack of biblicism, on the one hand, and disinterest in either the episcopacy or sacramental efficacy (such as, for example, baptismal regeneration), on the other, both problematize such classifications.

More work remains to be done. My hope is that this study shows Lewis in a new, if unexpected, light. The sources are, fittingly, both literary and theological. Just as we should expect. For once we begin to appreciate C. S. Lewis as a decidedly modern figure—the last of the Romantics—we discover layers upon layers to unpack, engage, and appreciate.

Appendix

POETIC FRAGMENTS
BY C. S. LEWIS

AT THE BACK OF C. S. LEWIS'S PERSONAL COPY of *The Shorter Poems of William Wordsworth: Poetry and Drama* (1917), he wrote a series of four, previously unpublished, poetic compositions.[1] The script, as confirmed by Lewis handwriting expert Charlie W. Starr, almost certainly dates to sometime between 1922 and 1924. The four inscriptions vary in length and meter, and the first two are each followed by a short dash at the margin. The third entry, a single line of verse, appears immediately after the second and is undoubtedly a stray, with no writing in the blank space beneath it. Last, the fourth selection appears at the top of the previous page and stops abruptly. Lewis may have intended these four writings as drafts or contributors to some future project.

The appearance of these poetic works at the back of *The Shorter Poems of William Wordsworth* is hardly a coincidence. Thematically he may have been inspired by Wordsworth's many well-known poems associated with death: "Ode: Intimations of Immortality," "We Are Seven," and "Surprised by Joy" all have death as a guiding

---

[1]Marginalia by C. S. Lewis, in William Wordsworth, *The Shorter Poems of William Wordsworth: Poetry and Drama*, Everyman's Library (London: Dent & Sons, 1917), rear verso free endpaper and inside rear recto flyleaf (C. S. Lewis Library collection, Wade). I wish to gratefully acknowledge David Downing, Laura Stanifer, and Charlie Starr for their insights and contributions to this transcription.

theme. During these years, Lewis had a growing admiration for Wordsworth—the greatest English poet since William Shakespeare and John Milton—and often spoke about his works. Lewis hoped one day to exceed Wordsworth in both skill and fame, particularly with the completion of his long poem *Dymer*, which he published in 1926 under the pseudonym Clive Hamilton. Although *Dymer* never earned Lewis the accolades he sought, he continued to write poetry (and read Wordsworth) throughout his life.[2]

The lines transcribed below reveal Lewis's creative imagination. The first selection is a particularly vivid example of Lewis's postwar restlessness. Readers will note his attention to Death personified and striking use of militaristic imagery. Given Lewis's reticence to reflect on the war in autobiographical works such as *Surprised by Joy*, these lines may clarify some of his private misgivings. The second selection is less emotive than the first, relying instead on patriotic references to an ancient past as the foundation for national fidelity. Yet, even amid such an appeal, the poet recognizes a disjunction between death and bloodshed imagined as a river and the vast incomprehensibility of a sea. Similarly, in the third and fourth inscriptions, Lewis intimates the stark gap between innocence and experience in matters of war.

In all, these four selections reveal sides of C. S. Lewis many readers have never encountered. Youthful Lewis, wrestling with death and dying. Scribbler of marginalia, engaging literature with a quick and capacious mind. War poet, grappling with combat in lines reminiscent of a Siegfried Sassoon or Wilfred Owen. In the marginalia at the back of a collection of Wordsworth's poetry, we discover C. S. Lewis once again.

---

[2]For the poem and its context, see Jerry Root, *Splendour in the Dark: C. S. Lewis's* Dymer *in His Life and Work*, ed. David C. Downing, Hansen Lectureship Series (Downers Grove, IL: IVP Academic, 2020); cf. *The Collected Poems of C. S. Lewis: A Critical Edition*, ed. Don W. King (Kent, OH: Kent State University Press, 2015).

[1]

They have gone in to the green arch of peace,
Death with finger on lip for them says Cease
To sun and moon and to the wind + rain:
Command the daybreaks all Come not again,
Death has rubb'ed out the sky, and sponged away
The whirligig of the whole coloured day
All in a moment. Death has called to heel
All sound: cut short the thunder in mid peel
Laid dumbness upon every tongue: the shout
Of millions like a puff'd flame is gone out
Follows the darkness closing like a chest,
No light, no sound, no thought, impartial rest
For each frayed sense. Oh never any more
Will cockcrow + reveille at their door
Come stirring. No hard duty shall have power
Forever to break on them for one hour

[2]

How conquerable was death
~~Before the world grew old~~
Before the iron age,
A pause in the firm heath
A turning of the page,
Such was our fathers faith
Before the world grew wise
Who, at the red hot stake
Sang Credo for Gods sake
Holding before their eyes
The deep fields of blue Paradise:
Who ^saw^ the eternal ramparts rise
Beyond the stream for death was then
A river and not yet a sea to men.

[3]

But these all for a crazy hundredth chance

[4]

Oh sweet shame of escape! He felt indeed
He had the big round world against his best,
His native star and trusty at his need.
The riot of his thoughts was laid to rest
And simply to lie breathing was the best
The load of thoughts

IMAGE CREDITS

1.1a. Photo of Morris Inch. Wheaton College Archives, Wheaton College, Wheaton, Illinois.

1.1b. Photo of Arthur Holmes. Wheaton College Archives, Wheaton College, Wheaton, Illinois.

1.1c. Photo of Clyde S. Kilby (1969). Kilby Papers Photos, call number: CSK / P-13. Used by permission of the Marion E. Wade Center, Wheaton College, Wheaton, Illinois.

1.2. Friedrich Schleiermacher, by Ernst Hader. In *The German Classics of the Nineteenth and Twentieth Centuries: Masterpieces of German Literature* (Albany, NY: J. B. Lyon, 1913). Wikimedia Commons.

1.3. Georg Wilhelm Friedrich Hegel, by Jakob Schlesinger (1831). Anagoria. Wikimedia Commons.

1.4. Sigmund Freud, by Max Halberstadt (ca. 1921). Wikimedia Commons.

1.5. Karl Marx, by John Jabez Edwin Mayal. In *Reminiscences of Carl Schurz* (New York: McClure, 1907), 1:170. Wikimedia Commons.

1.6. Marginalia by C. S. Lewis in Friedrich von Hügel, *Essays & Addresses on the Philosophy of Religion* (London: J. M. Dent & Sons, 1928), 97. C. S. Lewis Library collection, Marion E. Wade Center, Wheaton College, Wheaton, Illinois. © copyright CS Lewis Pte Ltd. Used by permission.

1.7. William Wordsworth, by William Shuter (1798). Wikimedia Commons.

1.8. Samuel Taylor Coleridge, by Peter Vandyke (1795). Wikimedia Commons.

2.1. *The Journal of Sarah Eliza Congdon.* Wheaton College Archives. Wheaton, Illinois.

2.2. Jacques Gérard Milbert, *Camp Meeting of the Methodists in North America* (ca. 1819). Wikimedia Commons.

2.3. William Hogarth, *Credulity, Superstition, and Fanaticism* (1762). Wikimedia Commons.

2.4. C. S. Lewis's personal copy of *John Wesley's Journal* (London: Isbister, 1902). C. S. Lewis Library collection, Marion E. Wade Center, Wheaton College, Wheaton, Illinois. Used by permission.

2.5. Title page, William Wordsworth, *The Prelude* (1850).

2.6. Benjamin Robert Haydon, *William Wordsworth on Helvellyn* (1842). Wikimedia Commons.

2.7. Marginalia by C. S. Lewis in S. T. Coleridge, *The Friend: A Series of Essays* (London: Bell & Daldy, 1865), 386 and verso of 389. C. S. Lewis Library collection, Marion E. Wade Center, Wheaton College, Wheaton, Illinois. © copyright CS Lewis Pte Ltd. Used by permission.

2.8. C. S. Lewis at Stonehenge, April 8, 1925. Wade call number: CSL-A / P-5. Used by permission of Marion E. Wade Center, Wheaton College, Wheaton, Illinois.

2.9. Title page of *The Golden String* by Bede Griffiths (London: Harvill, 1954). C. S. Lewis Library collection, Marion E. Wade Center, Wheaton College, Wheaton, Illinois. Used by permission.

2.10. Bede Griffiths, inscription to C. S. Lewis in *The Golden String* (1954). C. S. Lewis Library collection, Marion E. Wade Center, Wheaton College, Wheaton, Illinois. Used by permission.

2.11. Owen Barfield as a young man, ca. 1919–1925. OB / P-50. Used by permission of the Marion E. Wade Center, Wheaton College, Wheaton, Illinois.

2.12. Bede Griffiths. Used by permission of The Bede Griffiths Trust.

2.13. Bede Griffiths. Used by permission of The Bede Griffiths Trust.

2.14. Marginal inscription by C. S. Lewis in Coleridge, *The Friend*, 384-85. C. S. Lewis Library collection, Marion E. Wade Center, Wheaton College, Wheaton, Illinois. © copyright CS Lewis Pte Ltd. Used by permission.

2.15. Caspar David Friedrich, *Wanderer Above the Sea of Fog* (ca. 1817). Wikimedia Commons.

3.1. Lewis family wardrobe in the museum of the Marion E. Wade Center, Wheaton College, Wheaton, Illinois. Used by permission.

3.2. J. J. Dodd, C. Haghe, engraver, *Snowdon from Nantlle Lakes* (1854). Wikimedia Commons.

3.3. Marginalia by C. S. Lewis in Coleridge, *The Friend*, verso of table of contents. C. S. Lewis Library collection, Marion E. Wade Center, Wheaton College, Wheaton, Illinois. © copyright CS Lewis Pte Ltd. Used by permission.

3.4. Title page, *The Great Divorce* (1945). Courtesy of the Marion E. Wade Center, Wheaton College, Wheaton, Illinois.

3.5. Title page, S. T. Coleridge, "Kubla Khan" (1816). Wikimedia Commons.

3.6. John Keats, by William Hilton (ca. 1822). Wikimedia Commons.

3.7. Marginalia by C. S. Lewis in Coleridge, *The Friend*, 386 and verso of 389. C. S. Lewis Library collection, Marion E. Wade Center, Wheaton College, Wheaton, Illinois. © copyright CS Lewis Pte Ltd. Used by permission.

3.8. Title page, Joan Bennett, *Virginia Woolf: Her Art as a Novelist* (Cambridge: Cambridge University Press, 1945). C. S. Lewis Library collection, Marion E. Wade Center, Wheaton College, Wheaton, Illinois. Used by permission.

3.9. Marginalia by C. S. Lewis in Bennett, *Virginia Woolf*, front pastedown. C. S. Lewis Library collection, Marion E. Wade Center, Wheaton College, Wheaton, Illinois. © copyright CS Lewis Pte Ltd. Used by permission.

INDEX

The Marion E. Wade Center

Founded in 1965, the Marion E. Wade Center of Wheaton College, Illinois, houses a major research collection of writings and related materials by and about seven British authors: Owen Barfield, G. K. Chesterton, C. S. Lewis, George MacDonald, Dorothy L. Sayers, J. R. R. Tolkien, and Charles Williams. The Wade Center collects, preserves, and makes these resources available to researchers and visitors through its reading room, museum displays, educational programming, and publications. All of these endeavors are a tribute to the importance of the literary, historical, and Christian heritage of these writers. Together, these seven authors form a school of thought, as they valued and promoted the life of the mind and the imagination. Through service to those who use its resources and by making known the words of its seven authors, the Wade Center strives to continue their legacy.

The Hansen Lectureship Series

The Ken and Jean Hansen Lectureship is an annual lecture series named in honor of former Wheaton College trustee Ken Hansen and his wife, Jean, and endowed in their memory by Walter and Darlene Hansen. The series features three lectures per academic year by a Wheaton College faculty member on one or more of the Wade Center authors with responses by fellow faculty members.

Kenneth and Jean (née Hermann) Hansen are remembered for their welcoming home, deep appreciation for the imagination and the writings of the Wade authors, a commitment to serving others, and their strong Christian faith. After graduation from Wheaton College, Ken began working with Marion Wade in his residential cleaning business (later renamed ServiceMaster) in 1947. After Marion's death in 1973, Ken Hansen was instrumental in establishing the Marion E. Wade Collection at Wheaton College in honor of his friend and business colleague.